T0208315

Black Boys II Black Men

An Applied Dissertation Submitted to the
Abraham S. Fischler College of Education in
Partial Fulfillment of the Requirements for the
Degree of Doctor of Education

Dr. Cynthia D. Smith

authorHOUSE

AuthorHouse™
1663 Liberty Drive
Bloomington, IN 47403
www.authorhouse.com
Phone: 833-262-8899

Published by AuthorHouse 04/27/2023

ISBN: 979-8-8230-0701-6 (sc)
ISBN: 979-8-8230-0699-6 (hc)
ISBN: 979-8-8230-0700-9 (e)

Library of Congress Control Number: 2023907636

Nova Southeastern University
2018

Print information available on the last page.

This book is printed on acid-free paper.

APPROVAL PAGE

This applied dissertation was submitted by Cynthia D. Smith under the direction of the persons listed below. It was submitted to the Abraham S. Fischler College of Education and approved in partial fulfillment of the requirements for the degree of doctor of education at Nova Southeastern University.

Katrina Pann, PhD
Committee Chair

Steven Hecht, PhD
Committee Member

Kimberly Durham, PsyD
Dean

STATEMENT OF ORIGINAL WORK

I declare the following:

I have read the Code of Student Conduct and Academic Responsibility as described in the *Student Handbook* of Nova Southeastern University. This applied dissertation represents my original work, except where I have acknowledged the ideas, words, or material of other authors.

Where another author's ideas have been presented in this applied dissertation, I have acknowledged the author's ideas by citing them in the required style.

Where another author's words have been presented in this applied dissertation, I have acknowledged the author's words by using appropriate quotation devices and citations in the required style.

I have obtained permission from the author or publisher—in accordance with the required guidelines—to include any copyrighted material (e.g., tables, figures, survey instruments, or large portions of text) in this applied dissertation manuscript.

Cynthia D. Smith
_____
Name

October 1, 2018
_____
Date

ABSTRACT

Improving Reading Achievement Among African American Males in an Urban High School. Cynthia D. Smith, 2018: Applied Dissertation, Nova Southeastern University, Abraham S. Fischler College of Education. Keywords: reading achievement, culturally relevant education, parent participation, African American students.

Much has been written about reading disparities between African American males and other student groups. The purpose of this study was to examine the relationship between the reading achievement of African American males, particularly in high school settings, and specific factors that may support this achievement. Specifically, the relationship of reading achievement to parental involvement and culturally responsive instructional practices was considered. The expected outcome was to find correlations between African American parental involvement and reading achievement. It was also expected that culturally responsive teacher instructional practices would be correlated with student reading achievement.

A correlational research design was used, and data were collected from 227 participants. Research findings indicated significant correlations between reading achievement and (a) an attitude that all students are our students, (b) teacher collaboration to support all students, (c) availability of differentiated reading interventions, (d) consideration of a student's family situation by the instructional team, and (e) explicit instruction of learning strategies. Although these correlations were significant, it should be stressed that the associations between these variables and reading achievement were rather small, with correlations ranging between only .13 to .19 in magnitude. In addition, the remaining correlations reported in this study were so small that they did not pass the conventional levels of statistical significance.

Future research should provide needed information to assist today's educators and leaders in determining how to capture the unused academic potential of many African American male students. In addition, future research using qualitative research methods will enable the researcher to learn directly from students what factors African American male students associate with academic success as well as the challenges and solutions for achieving academic success.

ACKNOWLEDGEMENTS

Writing about something teaches you about what you know, what you don't know, and how to think about what you actually wrote. This book was a composition of my dissertation studies of what I have encompassed all my life seeing and experiencing the educational struggle of *Black Boys*. I hold an extreme interest in the need to improve the educational stigma which is the lack of academic achievement and barriers faced to succumb in impoverished environments. I want to dedicate this book to my son who is the first inspiration behind such intriguing topic. I want him to understand the research and the importance of going against the status quo and achieving academically beyond an expectation. My daughter deserves every accolade that this book receives, I spent her entire life researching and writing. My husband, I thank considerably for his patience that has kept me grounded and hopeful during uncertain times. Lastly, to every chairperson that believed in my research, gave feedback, and held my hand to the finish line "Thank you".

CONTENTS

References

Tables

Chapter 1

INTRODUCTION

Statement of the Problem

The outlook in today's schools regarding reading achievement among African American males is dismal (Casserly et al. 2012). In areas of high poverty, it is estimated that only one in ten African American students is on grade level in both reading and mathematics (National Center for Education Statistics 2011).

Based on federal, district, and state data, 53 percent of African American males do not graduate on time (Aarons 2010). Compared to African American females and Caucasian males, African American males have the highest dropout rates, poorest achievement rates, and lowest test scores in the nation (Butler, Shillingford, and Alexander-Snow 2011).

Children of color are at a higher risk of being represented in the lower ranges of the achievement gap (Greenwood 2011). Providing what amounts to an equitable education for African Americans and other minorities has been a persistent problem since the civil rights era and "subsequent federal and state antidiscrimination laws in the United States" (Kailin 2006, 649).

Although there have been reported gains in academic achievement among African American children, data from state and national levels suggest that reading-achievement gaps still exist (National Center for Education Statistics 2011). Poor reading achievement can prevent a solid, instructional foundation and disconnect students from successfully furthering their education (Blair 2009). Allington and Gabriel (2012) pointed out that children who haven't acquired the ability to read by second grade have a greater difficulty learning to read in later grades.

According to Tatum and Muhammad (2012), African American boys have historically faced dual circumstances of underachievement: being boys and being African American. Even when comparisons are made among African American students in general, there is a noted achievement gap between females and males within this group (White 2009).

Research has shown that a significant difference exists in the way boys and girls learn to read (Prado and Plourde 2011). Because learning to read is a process that develops over time and involves mastery of a variety of skills, it's important to know all the factors that can affect how a child becomes literate.

According to research, teachers should be knowledgeable of culturally sensitive and gender-based reading material for students to succeed (Kirkland 2011). Furthermore, the effect of practices related to academic achievement that teachers and parents utilize should be explored thoroughly through the context of research (Garrity 2009).

According to Kirkland (2011), culturally and socially sensitive literacy principles and instructional models are needed. These will assist in the continuing effort to help African American males rise from the academic abyss of low performance, a place that may intensify the social trauma many experience on any given day.

Kirkland stated, "A culturally and socially sensitive frame for literacy, thus, moves standards and instruction beyond the hegemonic past, but also keeps them from gravitating to other extremes, such as posturing literacy in Blackface" (2011, 374).

Gaps in student learning are the result of a student's inability to connect acquired knowledge to the broader elements of society, particularly the social, political, and economic components (Blair 2009). Various approaches to literacy lack social and cultural sensitivity and do little to recognize how African American youth, males in particular, actually practice literacy (Tatum 2006).

Traditionally, African American male students have not performed adequately on yearly state assessments across the nation (National Education Association 2011). And the disparities between African American male students and their Caucasian counterparts are drastic (Casserly et al. 2012). Parents and families represent a child's first teachers and have a powerful impact on their development.

Yet statistics show many African American males come from disjointed homes. The US Census Bureau (2012) indicated that 70 percent of African American children lived in single-parent homes. According to data analysis, African American males under eighteen years of age were three times more likely to live in a single-parent home than Caucasian children (Casserly et al. 2012).

Many single-parent African American families are economically unstable and face socioeconomic hurdles, such as a lack of transportation, limited communication skills, and low levels of literacy (Neely 2012).

Description of the Setting

This study's setting is a public high school in northern Florida. Located in the twenty-first largest urban school district in the state, the school has four main feeder middle schools. The site was established in 1928 and is therefore one of the oldest high schools in the city.

The school enrolls approximately eighteen hundred students and employs 120 staff members. The graduation rate for the district is 70 percent compared to the state's 78 percent (Florida Department of Education 2014). Many high school teachers report that teaching reading to at-risk students is overwhelming and daunting (Roney 2011). Several teachers at the research site are new and working to complete their reading certification, so they can earn their reading endorsement.

The problem is that, though 39 percent of all ninth-grade students were reading at levels of proficiency on the 2013 Florida Comprehensive Assessment Test (FCAT), only 29 percent of African American male students at the study site scored at the proficient level. This is compared to 65 percent of Caucasian males (Florida Department of Education 2014).

The student demographics at the site included 93 percent of the eighteen hundred students identifying as African American. The remaining 7 percent were a mixture of Caucasian and other races or ethnicities (Florida Department of Education 2014).

Probable Causes

Causes of poor reading development among African American males have been studied extensively. Studies have presented that they enter school already significantly behind their Caucasian peers in terms of vocabulary and fluency (Blair 2009).

Other scholars have attributed impaired reading achievement to low socioeconomic status (Tatum and Muhammad 2012), teacher attitudes and beliefs (Sheldon 2009), lack of parental support (Noguera 2008), and stereotypes that bolster social inequities. These then marginalize certain racial groups within the school setting (Kenyatta 2012).

Additionally, too many models have emphasized deficits in achievement between African American and Caucasian students. More research needs to be devoted to group studies of African American males using an achievement model (Graham and Anderson 2008).

Study Feasibility

In the existing setting, the researcher is responsible for monitoring students at risk of not graduating due to their inability to pass the reading section of the FCAT. The researcher has access to district and standardized assessments intended to monitor students' growth. These assessments include benchmark tests, such as the Florida Progress Monitoring and Reporting assessments in reading and previous FCAT data.

Analysis of this data was expected to give the researcher insight into the specific areas participants in the study struggled with. And it was to pinpoint areas for improvement throughout the study.

Background and Justification

The persistence of an achievement gap between Caucasian and African American children is problematic (Casserly et al. 2012). Challenging material in the secondary grades exacerbates the achievement-gap problem. And it continues with the disconnection of African American students from reading that could potentially improve their educational outcomes (Tatum 2008a, 2008b).

This study was used to explore potential ways to improve the existing reading outcomes of high school-aged African American males. There is a potential to replicate the findings of this study, which could serve as evidence of effective best practices for future research or school practices.

For example, Somers, Owens, and Piliawsky (2008) identified certain factors that contributed to the success or failure of African American children. Several of these factors, specifically the use of culturally relevant pedagogy and teaching, represent repetitive themes throughout the research (Olukolu 2013). Coggins and Campbell (2008) concluded that a culturally competent curriculum was necessary to close the achievement gap that persists among African American children.

This study was also used to focus on parents supporting the academic experiences of their children (Lee and Bowen 2006) as well as to determine the extent to which teacher involvement affected the students' levels of achievement (White 2009).

These approaches were further explored in participating classrooms at the local district level. It was to determine whether they provided a more holistic academic experience, particularly for African American boys, who are in urgent need of pedagogy that makes learning more meaningful (Tatum 2008a).

African American males in the district were not making competitive reading gains when compared to their Caucasian peers. Analyzing current state assessment reports shows there was a 36 percent difference in reading achievement (Florida Department of Education 2014).

These young males, often all too familiar with school-related failure, have been asked to meet expectations that are low or nonexistent (Garrity 2009). Moreover, through this study, pedagogical best practice strategies teachers used to help African American boys reach levels of proficiency in reading were examined (Blair 2009).

As Greenleaf and Hinchman (2009) stated, many adolescents are able to process textual information only at a literal level, which negatively affects their ability to comprehend text. Once pedagogical best-practice strategies are examined, results will be shared with district reading coaches in an effort to improve instruction and maximize the achievement of African American males.

Cultural Considerations

According to Holt and Smith (2005), socioeconomic and cultural factors interplay in the nonexistence of educational attainment. The existing factors are linked to the educational status of African American males across the United States. And at the school site for this study, the need for a curriculum that relates to students' lives is suggested (Gay 2010; Tatum 2008a, 2008b).

Therefore, educators should make an effort to ensure that students are not underrepresented in texts used in the classroom (Olukolu 2013). Ladson-Billings (2009) found that when teachers engaged in culturally responsive practices, student achievement increased significantly.

Furthermore, Tatum (2008a) argued that the achievement gap will not be closed unless effective reading strategies or literacy reform efforts are supplemented with meaningful texts African American males can connect and identify with.

Parent Participation

The push for African American boys to increase reading achievement is the mission at the writer's school. The research site is in an urban environment. And as research has shown, individual factors—such as socioeconomic status, nutrition, self-esteem and identity issues, and the level of parental participation in the child's education—are vital to a student's success (White 2009). Lopez (2011) theorized that the main reason African American males are less successful in the secondary school setting is that they lack support at home.

An effective way to help create changes in the learning issues for African American males would be to involve fathers or another male role model in their education (Brown 2009). At the research site selected for the dissertation study, several programs are geared toward involving fathers. One of the most notable programs is Watch D.O.G.S. (Dads of Great Students). Watch D.O.G.S. is an initiative to invite fathers to volunteer in the school for one day to involve African American male students' fathers in the education of their adolescent sons. However, it is well known at the research site that many of the fathers of those African American male students are absent, and many of them have uncles who are father figures in their lives.

Despite the potentially positive influence of their father figures, research suggests that children who do not live with their biological fathers do not perform as well academically as children who grow up with both biological parents in the home (Neely 2012). Parental support in the school environment is (a) identified through research as having a positive correlation to children's overall self-esteem, (b) necessary for the students to have a successful education (Mullins 2010), and (c) a very important aspect of this study. These factors are a critical part of improving the academic achievement of African American males (Brotherson and White 2007). Brown (2009) reported that parents' participation in their children's schooling frequently impacts the students' education in many positive ways including more than just academic achievement. Such measures (a) enhance children's self-esteem, (b) improve children's academic achievement, (c) improve parent-child relationships, (d) help parents develop positive attitudes toward school, and (e) give a better understanding of the schooling process.

Personal literacy behaviors. Most African American families do not have the means to subscribe to magazines and newspapers to enhance reading for pleasure compared to other minority groups (Harris and Duhon 1999). Engagement in these types of individual practices, such as reading books and newspapers, is known as personal literacy behavior. Research has shown that many African American children enter school with limited exposure to academic opportunities (Neely 2012; Piazza and Duncan 2012). According to Huang and Mason (2008), children who come from homes in which there is a strong emphasis placed on family literacy and parent involvement are more likely to be engaged in school, thus increasing their reading achievement (Sheldon 2009). In a study conducted by Senechal and Young (2008), results suggested that activities such as parent-child reading correlate to the development of a child's reading skills.

Teacher involvement. Moving past the identification of an achievement gap over the past fifty years, it has been determined that racial and ethnic cultures are factors in the assumptions, perceptions, and subsequent attitudes educators have toward their students (Kenyatta 2012). Many teachers are handicapped when it comes to motivating African American teenage males to read (Gregory, Skiba, and Noguera 2010; Kunjufu 2005; Noguera 2008). Teachers tend to struggle because they often do not understand the African American male or historical orientations that informed the reading practices of the African American male in the United States. Historical orientations of African American males' reading practices and contemporary voices of African American teenage boys inform us that teachers must discuss texts with African American male students in ways that lead toward a rich, optimal experience for these young men. Unfortunately, many African American teenage males have negative experiences in schools and do not encounter texts they find valuable (Noguera 2002, 2008). Educators increase the chances of motivating these young men to read by making informed text selections that are culturally relevant (Logan 2013).

To build awareness outside the classroom environment, educators and the community must work together to enhance learning. This effort includes working together for issues that include changing policies, creating new programs, and opening up new opportunities to actively engage African American males and their families in improving their personal outcomes. According to Noguera (2003), for these students to be successful, the work must also involve efforts to counter and transform cultural patterns that undermine the importance of education, which is a goal that can be achieved only if it is possible to provide alternative influences that offer a credible, realistic, and attractive source of hope and change.

Kozol (1991) explored how immensely different the educational experiences are between Caucasian middle-class students and poor minority students, particularly African Americans and Hispanics. Most studies surrounding the poor reading abilities of African American males identify the usual factors: (a) teacher quality, (b) parental involvement, and (c) after-school programs. Guthrie and Cambria (2011) pointed out that reading researchers are now faced with the task of focusing their attention on more significant ways to improve reading skills and increase reading achievement among African American students. Although exploratory studies have been designed to investigate the gap between high-ability and low-ability adolescent readers, along with decades of federal policy and mandates regarding reading instruction (Tatum and Muhammad 2012), none of this research has been designated specifically for African American children.

Deficiencies in the Evidence

Tatum and Muhammad (2012) posited that even the most aggressive education reform measures may not be sufficient enough to target the literacy development of African American boys. For example, there have been some indications through research that parents play an important role in school readiness and the academic achievement outcomes of young children (Joe and Davis 2009). In addition, other studies have shown that if African American males are to rise above low performance, culturally and socially responsive literacy practices and instructional models are needed to assist in the efforts (Kirkland 2011). This dissertation used quantitative measures to investigate (a) culturally relevant pedagogy, which includes instructional practices and teaching materials (Esposito and Swain 2009; Ladson-Billings 1995); and (b) parental involvement in the academic process and the impact of such involvement on the success of African American males (White 2009).

Definition of Terms

For the purpose of this applied dissertation, the following terms are defined:

Achievement gap. This term refers to the difference in academic performance among different ethnic groups (National Center for Education Statistics 2015).

Critical literacy. This term refers to learning to read and write as part of the process of becoming conscious of one's experience as historically constructed within specific power relations (Shor 2009).

Cultural instruction. This term defines culturally responsive teaching as using the cultural knowledge, prior experiences, and performance styles of diverse students to make learning more appropriate and effective for them; it teaches to and through the strengths of these students (Gay 2000, 2010).

Cultural literacy. This term refers to instruction that builds on cultural and linguistic backgrounds, ways of making meaning, and prior knowledge that all children bring to the classroom. Such instruction acknowledges the important role of culture in language and literacy learning. Understanding and respecting the array of different cultures and languages represented in their classrooms help educators to adopt strategies for teaching literacy that support student achievement (Tatum 2005).

Cultural responsiveness. As defined by Ladson-Billings (2009), culturally responsive practices are based on three standards: (a) student academic success, (b) the development of cultural competence, and (c) the establishment of a critical consciousness that allows students to question the status quo that exists in society.

Florida Comprehensive Assessment Test (FCAT). The term refers to the test that measures student success with state standards, including assessments in mathematics (i.e., grade ten and retake), science (i.e., grades five, eight, and even), and writing (i.e., grades four, eight, and ten) in the 2010–2011 school year. Historically, the FCAT measures the state standards in reading and mathematics (i.e., grades three to ten), science (i.e., grades five, eight, and eleven), and writing (i.e., grades four, eight, and ten). In this study, the researcher focused on the reading retake for African American males in grades eleven and twelve.

Free and reduced-price lunch. This term refers to a federally assisted meal program operating in public and nonprofit private schools and residential childcare institutions. It provides nutritionally balanced, low-cost, or free lunches to children each school day (Florida Department of Education 2014).

Personal literacy behaviors. This term refers to how children interact with books, articles, and reading material, such as book handling, recognizing, and imitating activities (Florida Department of Education 2014).

School readiness program. This term refers to a program that offers financial assistance to low-income families for early child's education and care so families can become financially self-sufficient and their young children can be successful in school in the future (Florida Department of Education 2014).

Self-image. This term refers to how individuals see themselves (Ladson-Billings 2009).

Audience

The audience for this study involves the students, parents, educational stakeholders, and teachers at the research site who participated in the study. Positively impacting this particular audience is important because achievement in literacy for African American males can promote collegial efforts, lower employment rates, and prevent incarcerations (Tatum and Muhammad 2012). Educators must work with parents to ensure that the most academically vulnerable students, such as African American boys, are nurtured and supported to maximize their academic potential (Mandara 2006). Whether for literacy or other subject areas, when parents are involved in their children's education, both children and parents are likely to benefit.

The conclusions of the study may be useful in conversations at the district level, in which efforts are centered on closing the achievement gap at the research site with district reading coaches, school administrators, and other stakeholders, who have a vested interest in the academic achievement of all learners. As African American males in high school continue to experience a decline in scoring above proficiency in reading, little has been done to address the contributing factors for this decline. Even when contributing factors are addressed, efforts are too generic to make any substantial impact (Tatum and Muhammad 2012). Emphasizing the importance of these factors can bring a new awareness to become a step closer to closing the achievement gap.

Purpose of the Study

This study's purpose was to examine the relationship between the reading achievement of African American males, particularly in high school settings, and specific factors that may support this achievement. Specifically, the relationship of reading achievement to parental involvement and culturally responsive instructional practices (Esposito and Swain 2009) was considered. Hill et al. (2011) proposed that positive racial identity and culturally responsive education are supportive of achievement in African American children.

Chapter 2

LITERATURE REVIEW

Introduction

This literature review presents various concepts that align with the purpose of this study. The historical perspective of this literature review provides an overview of the longstanding problems with literacy for African American males. The review summarizes recent data on the lack of improvement of these students on state and national tests as they continue to fall below average. In addition, as in any review of literature, it is important to research best-practice strategies other researchers have proven successful in their research so they may be adapted or modified for this specific study.

Theoretical Framework

To lay a foundation for this research study, several theories were examined as they related to the importance of culture in curriculum and the impact of a culturally responsive curriculum on the reading achievement of African American males. The principles of curriculum in the United States have always been largely Eurocentric (Greenwood 2011) or based on practices and beliefs of a European culture. However, such curriculum does not meet the needs of all learners, especially those who are unfamiliar with the experiences and principles of Eurocentrism. Attempts at cultural responsiveness within the curriculum have not met the standards for education when compared to the mainstream practices offered to middle- and upper-class Caucasian children (Ladson-Billings 2009).

Meier and Wood (2014) indicated that cultural responsiveness within the context of the American education system is a tool those in power use to remain in control of the academic environment by offering a compromise to those in opposition to the traditional curriculum. Although culture is generally infused as an add-on to the traditional curriculum, culturally responsive programs are courses taught outside of or within the formal classroom but are not considered part of the established curriculum to shape students' educational experiences (Kirkland 2011). As Troyna (1987) viewed it, the purported ethnic or cultural aspects of the multicultural ideology are blatant attempts to disguise the current Eurocentric curriculum.

According to supporters, culturally responsive education is designed to reduce those oppressive practices and ideologies commonly associated with minority groups in this country (Sleeter and Grant 2003). For boys, African American males specifically, their books are high interest but low level (Allington and Gabriel 2012). No longer are African American males rising to high expectations, but they are wallowing in low expectations. It is with a sigh that many educators determine that something must be done to correct years of dismal performance, but little is ever really done (Allington and Gabriel 2012). Colleagues often gather in teachers' lounges and shake their heads in confirmation as they swap stories about the lack of parental support and student behavior.

The problem child is likely to be an African American male whom everyone instantly knows by name or the boy whose name is an unwelcomed addition to the class roster (Allington and Gabriel 2012). True culturally responsive learning environments shift the focus from creating basic multicultural content to creating a classroom environment that emphasizes the cultural backgrounds of all students (Hughes 2010). In the framework of this study, culturally responsive learning was used as a foundation to explore ways in which educators could increase the literacy achievement of African American males in high school.

History of Reading Achievement for African American Males

Historical perspectives of African American male achievement are important not only to demonstrate the persistence of the problem but also to call into question why the problem continues to dominate the lives of African American males despite numerous research studies and theories that emerged from this issue (Blair 2009). Woodson (1933) questioned the authenticity of the education of African Americans in a Eurocentric culture, stating that, instead of being taught, African Americans were being indoctrinated to become inferior. Hughes (2010) pondered, "So then why, after all this time, when calculating the achievement of the 'American Dream,' are we still ranked at the bottom of almost every 'good' list, and at the top of the 'bad' lists?" (55). Other researchers had previously concluded that the American public education system linked the idea of the African American male with the term *disabled* (Kozol 1991).

According to Douglass and Baker (1982), Frederick Douglass stated, "Once you learn to read, you will be forever free" (11). This was a profound statement made during the time when many African Americans were enslaved and deprived of an education. Since the era of slavery, African American males have faced lifetimes of poor treatment and grave injustices. Once the prospect of education became within their reach, the longitude of injustice became even greater. Not only were they denied equal access to high academic standards long after the *Brown v. Board of Education* decision, but they also were systematically subjected to more referrals for disciplinary and special education referrals than any other group. Carmichael and Hamilton (as cited in Montero 2007) reported on the sluggish progress of desegregation. The achievement of African American males in reading continues to fall far below expectations on an annual basis, which raises red flags among politicians and educators with passive interest but without any aggressive efforts to actively implement change.

Although there has been some progress in the educational opportunities afforded African American children, their achievement levels continue to lag behind even the poorest of Caucasian children. The African American community has long considered education to be a top priority (Hamilton

15

2009) and somewhat of a means to a better life and greater aptitudes for success. Greater emphasis within the community has been placed on the push for African American males to graduate from high school, although their graduation rates fall below the national standard. Without the basic support of a high school diploma, the African American male faces reduced prospects of going to college or obtaining any means of gainful employment that will allow him to be successful among his peers (Stevans 2009).

It has been reported that the overall number of high school students who read at or above proficiency has been on a downward slope since 2002 (National Center for Education Statistics 2010). Garrity (2009) related that in the area of reading, African American students are losing opportunities to gain fundamental skills that will determine their successes or failures later in life. In 2013, the Education Trust reported that African American students graduating from high school had math and reading skills that were comparable to those of eighth-grade Caucasian students. Low levels of reading performance of African American males have been narrowly investigated (Aarons 2010). Low literacy levels lead to poorer trajectories and limit the ability of African American males to gain the information they need to succeed in the workplace (Educational Testing Service 2011). Their opportunities in life are greatly reduced, and the potential for failure becomes more of a reality than the potential to excel.

Further Research

Further research to explore the perceptions and lived experiences of African American males regarding their reading achievement is highly recommended. This research study contributes empirical evidence that supports previous research on reading achievement during middle childhood (i.e., ages nine to eleven). Using prior research as a foundation, researchers have provided additional insights on African American males' cultural forms, attitudes, and styles of behavior that can diminish the importance of academic achievement in reading, which can further hinder their academic success in reading. Such emphasis is appropriate because research on effective schools has shown that when optimal conditions for teaching and learning are provided, high levels of academic success for students, including African American males, can be achieved (Duke et al. 2011).

It is important to acknowledge that, in addition to the issues discussed in this paper, many other factors and variables require an examination to gain a deeper understanding of how to improve the reading achievement of African American students, such as the educational environment, school setting, and physical and emotional characteristics of students (Averitt 2011). Conducting research in traditional school settings has become increasingly difficult in this era of accountability. Districts often mandate both general instructional policies and specific reading curricula, making it more difficult to introduce new approaches. This may suggest the need for a more ethical approach to conduct research in large urban school districts, an approach that provides direct benefits to students, as evident by improved reading and writing scores. The need for such research is urgent for African American male adolescents.

Finally, in the future, the effectiveness of reading research will be measured in terms of its ability to produce empirical findings that influence the development of curriculum materials, educational programs, and innovative approaches that yield significant gains in reading achievement for African American male students. Although several scholars have contributed greatly to the research literature on matters pertaining to African American students and reading (Edwards 2004; Entwisle and Alexander 1988; Flowers 2003; Hale 2001), additional research is needed to examine in greater detail the factors that influence the achievement of these students. Furthermore, research is needed to support the development of appropriate strategies and dispositions required for African American students to become proficient readers. Using this as a foundation for further study, this literature review provides a brief discussion of the trends in literacy as well as trends among African American males and their performance, value in education, mentoring programs, and best-practice strategies to enhance their academic achievement.

Factors Linked to Low Literacy Levels

Several factors have been found to contribute to poor literacy achievement when it comes to African American students. No single factor can be cited as the sole cause of reading failure among African American students. However, those variables that do contribute to poor literacy are most often associated with socioeconomics, including poverty, and have been found to have a greater effect on student achievement (Lopez 2011). This finding is relative to the study of poor achievement among African American children because they are five times more likely than their peers to live in conditions in which poverty is commonplace (US Census Bureau 2012).

African American teens who live in poverty face a greater probability of not graduating from high school (Banks and Oliveira 2011). Research has further suggested that African American males are almost twice as likely as Caucasian males not to graduate from high school, with 9 percent for the former and 5 percent for the latter (Banks and Oliveira 2011). Data from the National Assessment of Educational Progress (National Center for Education Statistics 2015) showed only a 14 percent or above proficiency rate for African American children on eighth-grade national reading tests.

Recent Relevant Data

The National Center for Education Statistics (2013) reported a disparity, known as an achievement gap, in reading scores in America. The achievement gap can be defined as the difference between the average scores of various student groups. According to Heckman (2011a), African American males on many measures perform worse than Caucasians overall. Although numerous influences contribute to the lack of academic success, these barriers can be a reflection of the future African American males may face in postsecondary education. Only 54 percent of African Americans graduate from high school compared to more than three-quarters of Caucasian and Asian students (Heckman 2011a, 2011b).

Spellings (2012) stated, "Half of our minority students don't graduate from high school on time, and millions of students move through the system without having basic reading and math skills" (C-3). It can be reasonably concluded that the millions of students to whom Spellings was referring are African Americans. This group has historically faced challenges related to low academic and societal expectations, culturally irrelevant instructional practices, inequity in disciplinary processes and procedures, lower referrals for academically gifted classes, and disproportionate placement in special education classes within public school systems across America (Ford and Moore 2013).

Researchers at the Advancement Project found that approximately seven out of every ten students graduate from high school, with New Jersey being the only state in the union to boast a graduation rate for African American male students greater than 65 percent (Jenkins 2009). The Schott Foundation for Public Education (Aarons 2010) reported that even in five of the best districts within the American public school structure, African American males are graduating at a rate of only 10 to 31 percent when compared to their Caucasian male counterparts. In the future, though graduation rates may improve, the gaps may actually increase (Aarons 2010).

According to the National Center for Education Statistics (2015), high school graduation rates for African Americans were about 54 percent when compared to more than three-quarters of Caucasian and Asian students who graduate from high school. On a national average, African American males were approximately 2.5 times as likely as Caucasian students to be suspended from school across all grade levels. These statistical averages are critical when it is estimated that roughly $260,000 is lost in earnings, taxes, and other revenue for every student who does not graduate from high school.

According to the National Assessment of Educational Progress (National Center for Education Statistics 2013), in 2012 African American students at the twelfth-grade level scored lower on the reading assessment than any other minority group. The results of the grade-twelve scores on the reading assessment indicate the importance of teachers and parents of African American students. This information is needed to understand how test results should be used to inform future practice regarding the education of these students, particularly the need to seek the most practical human and fiscal resources to improve the reading skills of African American students. After teachers gain an understanding of where students come from as a result of testing data, they can incorporate learning styles, culture, background, prior knowledge, and vocabulary into the curriculum.

The reading portion of the National Assessment of Educational Progress measures reading ability in three areas: (1) literary experience, (2) information, and (3) task performance. Moreover, the assessment measures four additional aspects of reading: (1) forming a general understanding, (2) developing interpretation, (3) making reader-to-text connections, and (4) examining content and structure. Taking the results of the test and further analyzing African American students' performance on individual measures of reading ability within the assessment may shed additional light on the areas in which they struggle the most and allow educators to strategically plan how to target these specific areas to improve the reading ability of African American students.

Over a decade ago, Flowers (2003) explored how reading for pleasure influenced students' reading achievement. Overall, the study results supported the idea that reading for pleasure has a positive correlation to the scores of African American students on standardized reading assessments; most notably the amount of time spent reading outside of school had the greatest impact on student reading achievement. Further analysis of the results associated large percentages of African American seniors who read for pleasure and scored at level two and level three on standardized reading assessments. Based on the findings of the research study, one could arguably advise that students should have an opportunity to select reading material outside of school to increase their scores on standardized reading assessments.

Likewise, educators may want to consider the link between reading for pleasure and literacy development outcomes indicated in the study when planning and implementing homework assignments for African American students. Similar findings were replicated in the US Department of

Education's (2012) research evidence on reading for pleasure. An important point regarding students reading for pleasure is that it gives them the opportunity to become transformative. Being transformative involves helping "students to develop the knowledge, skills, and values needed to become social critics who can make reflective decisions and implement their decisions in effective personal, social, political, and economic action" (US Department of Education 2012, 131). Culturally responsive teaching enables students to be better human beings and more successful learners.

Reading Achievement

Tatum (2006) suggested that an achievement gap could be calculated by taking the difference between high and low academically performing students based on their standardized reading and math assessment scores, their academic placement at both the middle and high school levels, and their grade point averages. GPAs are not represented equitably because of ambiguous academic performance standards and inconsistent assessments that fail to comprehensively represent students' academic abilities. The author also discussed the dismal academic performance of African American adolescent males that ultimately leads to their disproportionate placement in special education programs or assignment to lower-level reading and math courses, in which low expectations and lack of academic rigor often lead them to drop out of high school after years of consistent failures.

Existing research has shown that Caucasian males consistently outperform African American males in reading achievement in elementary school, which indicates a predictor of outperformance in high school (Lewis et al. 2010). Because reading achievement among African American males continues to decrease, however, researchers have examined factors that contribute to this trend, one of which is that African American students perform better with African American teachers (Center on Education Policy 2012; US Department of Education 2012; White 2009).

Incorporating Culturally Relevant Literature

American public schools are seemingly still indifferent when it comes to responding to the poor conditions for minorities and disadvantaged children (Blair 2009). If educators and policy makers are to make progress in addressing the occurrence of systematic racism within the school setting, reflection on culture cannot be avoided during the process (Wood and Jocius 2013). In fact, Nichols and White (2001) posed the critical question, asking how educators could become more sensitive to different cultures. In the field of education, cultural responsiveness emphasizes the importance of acknowledging that it is necessary to infuse elements of culture into the curriculum if students are to benefit from their academic experiences (Dee and Jacob 2011). Ladson-Billings (2009) and Gay (2010) insisted that educators can effectively raise achievement levels among minority and low-income children by using the cultural and linguistic strengths of these students in the learning process, thus validating their interests in the learning process.

There have been multiple studies that support effective instructional practices and culturally relevant pedagogy as a means of decreasing the achievement gap experienced by African American students (Garrity 2009). When teachers select relevant reading materials, African American adolescent males become more engaged in the text and develop skills, strategies, and knowledge that can improve their outcomes (Tatum 2006). The types of reading materials made available in the classroom may contribute to the disinterest that students demonstrate (Olukolu 2013). Teaching grounded in the tenets of cultural relevance must acknowledge the reading cultures of students in the classroom (Gay 2000, 2010; Ladson-Billings 1995, 2009). If all students are to have a chance at success regardless their culture or background, teachers are challenged to find ways to meet the needs of all learners (Heckman 2011a, 2011b). It has been noted that curriculum and instruction that include culturally relevant topics are found to heighten motivation and student engagement (Greenwood 2011; Holloway 2006; Li 2011; Noguera 2002, 2003, 2008, 2012).

Increasing Parent Participation

The family serves as the foundation of learning for children. A growing body of research has correlated an increase in student academic performance and parent involvement in the child's education (Epstein 2008, 2011; Hayes 2011; Huang and Mason 2008; Raftery, Grolnick, and Flamm 2012). Additional studies have addressed parental involvement in schools and its impact on student academic growth (Hill and Tyson 2009; Hines and Holcomb-McCoy 2013). Stewart (2007) conducted a longitudinal study by interviewing all stakeholders including students, parents, and educators over a two-year period. In Stewart's study, analyses were based on data collected from 546 high schools with approximately twelve hundred African American students. Within this student population, 52 percent of the students were females.

As part of the study, student participants were asked to indicate how often their parents or guardians were involved in school-related activities that included attending school meetings or volunteering in the school. Students were also asked to indicate the extent of their parents' or guardians' involvement in activities, such as course or program selection at school. Overall, results from the study pointed to a direct relationship between student achievement and positive parental involvement. The more involved parents were in their child's school-related activities, the more committed that child was to his or her schoolwork (Stewart 2007).

When parents engaged in discussions with their child about academics, a significant association with the child's academic success was found (Ortiz 2001). Children who are engaged in discussions with their parents about school appear to be more likely to see higher grade point averages (Ortiz 2001). Hayes (2011) proposed that educators and administrators must do more to involve parents in the education process if student achievement is truly a top priority. Strategies such as the creation of a school-wide parent, teacher, and student organization or school-based parent forum sessions that allow families to discuss their concerns about education could be used to promote open lines of communication between school and home. This type of strategy would likely improve student achievement through increases in parent involvement. Therefore, the researcher planned to create a school-wide parent, teacher, and student organization like this to increase parental engagement, ultimately increasing student achievement.

Parental Involvement and Student Reading Achievement

Parental involvement can be broadly defined as parents' support of their children in the school environment to ensure that their children progress academically (Hill and Tyson 2009). Several studies have shown increased academic achievement for children whose parents were involved in their education (Arnold et al. 2008; Hill and Tyson 2009; Senechal and Young 2008). Supportively, sixteen studies of parental involvement demonstrated a positive correlation between parental support and children's reading attainment (Senechal and Young 2008). Despite the establishment of strong correlational data indicating the connection between parental support and higher student academic achievement, it should be noted that parental influence and involvement in adolescents' lives diminish with age (Epstein 2005).

Some of the factors identified as detriments to African American student achievement include (a) low socioeconomic conditions, (b) single-parent households, (c) parental involvement in education (Epstein 2011), and (d) parental expectations and beliefs (Wu and Qi 2006). For example, research has suggested that African American parents have higher expectations and involvement with their daughters, with females showing higher graduation rates than their male counterparts (Nebbitt et al. 2009). Likewise, parents from lower socioeconomic status are less likely to have any significant involvement in their children's education for several reasons, including mistrust of the education system, personal school failure, and poor communication between the school and home (Lopez 2011).

Hayes (2011) used this as a catalyst for examining two groups of African American parents from a range of socioeconomic backgrounds in urban environments. The author sought to understand how these parents perceived various situations associated with the school environment. All parents in the study had children who were in high school. Results were used to predict the level of involvement these parents were most likely to have concerning their child's education. The first group of parents consisted mostly of low-income and working-class members of the community. The second group was composed of low-income and upper-middle-class parents from the community. The results revealed that, although these parents lived in urban environments, they reported having very high aspirations for their children's academic success. More specifically, 86 percent of the parents who participated in both study groups expressed a desire for their children to attend and subsequently graduate from college.

Further, researchers have suggested that there is a relationship with future academic achievement when parents communicate their expectations to their adolescents by empowering them to set and maintain educational goals (Epstein 2005, 2008 2011; Hill and Tyson 2009). The assessments used to determine performance were the pretests and posttests administered to the participating students at the research site. The impact of parental involvement in the education of their children has been documented in several research studies (Epstein 2005, 2008, 2011; Hayes 2011; Hill and Tyson 2009). Although the research doesn't pinpoint the types of parental involvement that are most conducive to student success, it does correlate positive relationships between home and school as being a primary predictor of student outcomes (Hayes 2011).

Within the context of parental involvement, the issue of socioeconomics was considered a subfactor. The academic achievement of African American male adolescents is critically influenced by their social environment (Martin et al. 2007). The home lives of African American males tend to be quite different from those of their Caucasian peers in many respects (Watson, Kehler, and Martino 2010). This is important because there has been some suggestion that students from lower socioeconomic environments do not have significant amounts of parental support when it comes to their education.

This is a critical point because, using previous research findings as a basis, we see that these students will not perform well in school and will likely be among the poorest readers in the classroom. Teachers and administrators assume that poor or minority parents who are not actively involved in their children's education do not care about their children's success (Casserly et al. 2012). The more involved parents are in school functions, parent-teacher meetings, and other school-related activities, the more positively school personnel view parents (Hill et al. 2011). In other words, African American males whose families do not support their academic experiences will not have the greatest potential to succeed.

Although the issue of parental involvement has been studied extensively through various research reports (Edwards 1992, 2004; Ortiz 2001; Roberts, Jurgens, and Burchinal 2005) and exploratory articles, there has not been much research to determine which types of parent involvement served as the most suitable when it came to supporting African American male achievement in school. This area of study has not been a priority when it comes to studying African American children in urban environments (Hughes 2010; Noguera 2008).

Parental Level of Education

Taking the time to read to their children is an essential activity for parents related to their child's ability to succeed in the classroom. Korat (2011) examined the relationship between mothers and their children's literacy levels. The mothers were evaluated based on their interactions with their children's literacy activities in high socioeconomic settings. To determine the parents' socioeconomic status group, researchers used the mother's education level as part of their equation. Korat suggested that education level could be an accurate predictor of children's literacy levels regardless of whether the mother had a high or low level of education. When examining specific factors such as parental involvement, Epstein (2008) found that parents who had more education had a higher probability of being involved in their children's education; however, according to Epstein, this was not a meaningful predictor of how well their children would do at school. This is a different perspective than that offered by Korat and other researchers, who pointed directly to parental involvement and student success in the classroom.

Conceptually, parental involvement is a complex phrase that encompasses a variety of parental behaviors, such as reading to children, attending school activities, and actively participating in extracurricular activities (Fashola 2013). Parents who are involved in their children's education are more likely to play a crucial role in their child's success in reading. The more involved the parents are in their child's reading activities, the more successful the child will be. Parents who are also active readers will likely motivate their children to want to read. The degree to which parents are involved in their children's schooling has been directly linked to positive educational outcomes (Fashola 2013). The academic achievement of African American males could feasibly be linked to a number of factors that both positively and negatively influence their outcomes.

One factor that has consistently been present in research related to higher levels of academic achievement has been parents' participation in the education processes involving their children (Topor et al. 2010). Parental involvement has been a much-debated topic as educators and politicians argue about its importance in connection to the achievement gap existing between Caucasian and African American students (Blair 2009). Further research is needed to ascertain those methods that are most effective in increasing parental involvement, which will subsequently lead to an increase in student reading achievement (Whitaker et al. 2012), more specifically in the African American community, which has been identified as one of the areas where such an environment is lacking.

Reading underachievement among African American boys in elementary school leads to poor academic outcomes in high school, reduced educational attainment, and delinquency (Hill and Tyson, 2009). Sullivan (2010) conducted a study using data from the Early Childhood Longitudinal Study-Kindergarten cohort to examine the relationship between cultural capital transmission and reading achievement within a nationally representative sample of fifth-grade African American males. Logistic regression techniques were used to examine several differences between high-achieving and low-achieving African American male students. Regression analyses were used as controlling factors for third-grade achievement, family structure, socioeconomic status, and parental involvement. The findings indicated that parent-supervised artistic activities including dance, music, fine arts lessons, and live theater are related to positive academic development, whereas artistic activities supervised by other adults are not. As parents spent time with their sons in museums, libraries, zoos, aquariums, and related places, boys' literacy scores improved.

Similar to the limitations in the dissertation research, the existing findings of this study have significant implications regarding public policy that may improve the achievement of African American boys. However, it appears that parents with limited financial resources are less likely to visit these sites. Although financial resources are positively associated with cultural capital, it is unclear what other factors contribute to this relationship. In addition to limited resources, there is likely a lack of awareness of how these activities contribute to children's cognitive development.

The early socialization of children regarding the values of education begins with parental expectations and beliefs about what academic achievement necessitates (Wood, Kurtz-Costes, and Copping 2011). Parents who have high expectations for their children encourage them to have high expectations for themselves and establish plans for their children's future education (Hines and Holcomb-McCoy 2013). Parents who have succeeded academically have more leverage to encourage their children to succeed academically and take action to help their children succeed (Gantt and Greif 2009). Research also suggests two-parent families may be able to provide more resources, more supervision, and greater stability than single-parent families (Gantt and Greif 2009). Children from single-parent families are more likely to perform poorly on tests and exhibit more behavioral problems in school than children from two-parent families (Lewis et al. 2010). Socioeconomic status is the best predictor of attainment (Lewis et al. 2010); however, when race is factored in, socioeconomic status has been shown to be a weak explanation for differences in academic achievement (Gantt and Greif 2009).

Teaching Critical Literacy Skills

Critical literacy is the process by which an individual actively engages in the exploration and discussion of underlying assumptions that exist within the context of literary works or in other mediums (McLaughlin and DeVoogd 2014). Engagement in critical literacy serves as an effective means for helping children become more formidable readers (Stevens and Bean 2007). For example, critical literacy could help children develop an awareness of how people or events are portrayed within the context of a literary work. Once students become more engaged in the process of critical literacy or as they are learning how to read and write as a means of developing self-realization about their individual experiences, they become more aware of the historical constructions that are specific to certain relationships of power (Vasquez, Tate, and Harste 2013). During this process, they also become more aware of how their views shape the manner in which they interpret texts and how they interact with other people (Vasquez, Tate, and Harste 2013).

According to Tatum (2008a), critical literacy practices should help teachers and students expand their reasoning, seek out multiple perspectives, and become active thinkers. A case study presented by Hall and Piazza (2008) analyzed the critical literacy skills of three African American male students. Each participant engaged in sessions in which he was asked to read and discuss four texts over a three-week period. Each text was differentiated based on social, cultural, and linguistic contexts. An audiotaped read-aloud session of a fictional text was provided, and each student followed along by silently reading the text. The texts contained themes such as discrimination or social conflicts based on race or lack of conformity to societal expectations.

After completing the text reading, the boys were interviewed and asked to interpret the text. Subsequently, the boys' interpretations of the text were then analyzed to determine the influence that these interpretations had on the boys' cultural understanding of characteristics that define manhood. Each participant expressed common characteristics that they attributed to the male image in society. As a result, Hall and Piazza (2008) suggested that educators incorporate more critical literacy skills into the classroom to support students' engagement in the critical literacy process; as a result, these students can make a conscious effort to shape their beliefs about the world.

Morris (2011) believed that maximized learning was predicated on three activities. The first activity, demonstration, questions what can be done and how. McCullough (2013) noted that strategies represent a road map that shows students the process by which something is done. Hartney and Flavin (2014) supported this idea, stating that strategies should be conscious plans of action developed to help students achieve a goal. The authors also suggested that strategies could be adapted to a particular situation.

The second activity, engagement, according to Morris (2011), is the manner in which the learner actively connects with the activity. An example of engagement may be how the reader pauses to make connections with the text. He or she may identify something in the reading that he or she has experienced on a personal level; or he or she may note that the text is similar in some way to another text he or she has previously read. In these instances, engagement has occurred because the student has engaged in the reading by using his or her background knowledge about the text. Regardless of the perceived difficulty of the reading task, the student is interested enough in the content to remain engaged in the reading (Hartney and Flavin 2014).

The final activity Morris (2011) identified involves sensitivity. The author noted that learning is not guaranteed simply because the learner made a personal effort to learn or because of the learner's personal motivation to learn; rather, learning takes place through vicarious observations. Along with observations, Guthrie and Cambria (2011) encouraged collaborations in which students were able to generate questions based on class discussions. By exploring questions related to the reading of a text, students were able to support each other to broaden their understanding of the text.

Value in Education

African Americans often see the attainment of education as a means of both social status and economic prosperity (Boone, Rawson, and Vance 2010). When comparing results from data obtained from standardized tests, researchers found that African Americans have systematically underperformed on these tests when compared to their Caucasian and Asian American peers. According to Boone, Rawson, and Vance (2010), ecological factors, such as environment and personal background, are causal factors in determining the level of success an African American child will have in school. In another study by Guest and Schneider (2013), there was a correlation made between high school students' participation in various extracurricular activities (e.g., sports and interest clubs) and an increase in their achievement levels. In a study by Nebbitt et al. (2009), peer associations are noted as important for academic achievement among adolescents.

Moreover, when adolescents form relationships with peers who are interested in their education and strive for academic success, those adolescents have an increased interest in school as well and invest more of their time and efforts toward conforming to school-based expectations (Crosnoe et al. 2010). The school environment either motivates students to learn or causes them to lose interest in the learning process altogether. The structure of the school is most indicative of students' success or failure, particularly the manner in which the school builds its staff, organizes its resources, and maintains either a positive or negative climate (Waters, Cross, and Shaw 2010).

Dawkins, Braddock, and Celaya (2008) noted that most African American boys seem to be interested in sports, action, and technology. Wood and Jocius (2013) pointed out that classroom-based literacy instruction is often designed based on a monotone curriculum without regard to the social, cultural, and personal influences related to the African American reader and writer. Students, adolescents in particular, say too often, "I hate this stupid book!" and "These books are dumb anyway." Wood and Jocius believed that the solution to these issues lay in three areas: (a) culturally relevant texts, (b) collaboration, and (c) critical conversations.

Culturally relevant texts are used to make instructional decisions about the types of literary works that can be used to successfully engage racially, ethnically, culturally, and linguistically diverse student populations in the reading process. These types of texts pay homage to students' personal experiences and those things that are most relevant to their everyday living. Characters, plots, themes, and dialogue are relatable, increasing students' ability to understand the context of the stories they are reading. Collaboration gives students shared ownership in their literacy development by allowing them to have a voice in their own learning. When teachers incorporate their students' ideas and experiences into the instructional process, students become more engaged because they understand their teacher has a genuine interest in their success. Critical conversations provide a safe, respectful platform for students to share their ideas and question the ideas of others. The critical conversation piece is used as a means of developing critical thinking, not as a method of degrading or insulting another individual's beliefs.

Mentoring Programs

Even though the researcher was not utilizing mentoring programs as a best-practice strategy for the current study, it was essential to include a variety of the most used strategies when researching a topic. Research has indicated that African American males benefit from mentoring programs (Hughes 2010). Findings from Gordon et al. (2009), for example, supported the use of mentoring programs as a means of promoting academic achievement among African American boys at the middle school level. The findings suggest that students do not have a clear understanding of ways they can engage students outside their intimate social groups.

Additionally, mentoring programs have been shown to benefit those students who are actively involved in the mentorship. Few studies have empirically investigated how mentoring programs positively impact academic achievements among African American male students. There have been few empirically grounded research studies devoted to the relationship between mentorships and academic achievement among African American males. These studies could support an increase in the implementation of such programs if they are shown to significantly impact academic achievement for young African American males.

Model mentoring programs, such as the one the Benjamin E. Mays Institute offered, create a foundation for achievement by underscoring the underachievement of young African American males and focusing on ways these adolescent boys can be nurtured and groomed for success. The model emphasizes Afrocentrism, positive socialization, cultural identity, and single-gender classroom instruction. Findings from a sample of sixty-one adolescent African American males at the middle school level indicated that there was a statistically significant difference in achievement scores among participants in the Benjamin E. Mays Institute program when compared to males who did not participate in the mentoring program.

Teacher Involvement

Teaching has become less autonomous because teachers are not being given the flexibility necessary to create lessons that reflect their personal teaching styles and preferences. Many teachers are now required to use scripted teaching guides and materials that are less about creativity and more about structured, automated responses to instruction (Karchmer-Klein and Shinas 2012). Despite an overemphasis on testing and results-driven curricula, the Bill and Melinda Gates Foundation (Kane and Staiger 2012) pointed to a study involving more than forty thousand teachers, in which a majority of participants indicated that norm-referenced tests were not appropriate measures of student performance. Approximately 89 percent of the participants felt that students were more successful when they were exposed to curriculum that went above and beyond what was on the standardized tests (Kane and Staiger 2012). Teaching to the test was ill advised; it did not create a standard by which student learning was adequately measured, and there was no evidence that students benefited from such instruction. Participants indicated that the rigor and relevance of the curriculum had a more profound impact on student achievement (Kane and Staiger 2012).

A lack of meaningful professional development has negative implications on teachers who need support to improve their ability to be effective teachers in the classroom. Overemphasis on test scores not only takes away from their ability to develop their skills in the classroom but also creates an environment in which students are being trained more so to become test takers as opposed to becoming successful, engaged learners. Meier and Wood (2014) pointed directly to the No Child Left Behind Act as a causal factor for the current state of education in this country. The quality of education, according to the authors, has declined considerably, teachers have become test-taking practitioners, and students are less engaged because their learning experiences lack authenticity.

Instead of overemphasizing the importance of state-level testing, Ford and Moore (2013) suggested placing greater weight on finding ways to improve classroom instruction as the only manner to increase student achievement. Graves and Howes (2011) noted that professional development was a warranted investment in preparing more effective teachers in the classroom. Professional-development activities should be based on current practices and trends in education, requiring teachers to learn those instructional approaches that have been researched and confirmed to be the most efficient practices for increasing student achievement.

High Expectations

The high expectation for culturally, linguistically, racially, or ethnically minority students to succeed is not a negotiable practice (Gay 2000). Teachers must believe without a doubt that all students can achieve (Au 2006, 2011). Demanding the best from students, White (2009) argued, educators must challenge students to reach greatness if the overall goal of education is to raise achievement levels for those students who have historically been prone to poor academic performance outcomes because of their minority status.

A commitment to higher expectations for students should begin long before teachers enter the classroom. Teacher in-service and preservice programs should dedicate ample time to focus on the correlations between teachers' expectations and perceptions, and student academic achievement. It is advisable for preservice and professional-development programs to incorporate cultural competency training, specifically as it relates to African American males, because research supports positive outcomes for students when their teachers believe they are capable of doing well academically. More specifically, preservice and in-service training programs need to focus on creating an awareness of cultural differences that may affect the student-teacher relationship and cause a misinterpretation of behaviors based on preconceived ideas or experiences related to culture. Furthermore, training may prove more beneficial by focusing on effective cultural strategies to support increases in academic achievement.

Much of the literature concerning the education of young African American males emphasizes the need for professional development designed to bring awareness to teachers' instructional practices as well as teachers reflecting their own views about culture, biases about other cultures, and their attitudes concerning African American males (Turney and Kao 2009). Furthermore, Dee and Jacob (2011) examined the impact of No Child Left Behind on instructional practices within the classroom, particularly on those practices that placed greater emphasis on standardized test results, which has contributed to attitudes and behaviors of indifference among African American students.

Dee and Jacob (2011) reached these conclusions based on data collected from a questionnaire and a focus group composed of African American, Latino, and Caucasian students at a low-performing high school. Many items from the questionnaire focused on the beliefs of student participants regarding curriculum, teachers, and standardized testing. Findings indicated that African American and Latino students were more likely than Caucasian students to be dissatisfied with their teachers and the quality of instruction. Additionally, results revealed that 66 percent of the African Americans participating in the questionnaire found the curriculum to be irrelevant compared to 57 percent of Latinos and 48 percent of Caucasian students who participated in the study. Schools that have a high enrollment of African American students must reexamine the way they operate and determine whether improvements need to be made to their infrastructure (Dee and Jacob 2011). African American children need high-quality, dedicated, and effective teachers to be successful in school. Previous studies revealed that there is a significant relationship between teacher effectiveness and African American student achievement (Garrity 2009).

Moreover, Boone, Rawson, and Vance (2010) expressed that educators needed to further examine the manner in which ideas of masculinity are constructed within the African American community. It would seem that ideas of masculinity are largely based on media representations and preexisting observations concerning traditional or dominant roles that are synonymous with masculinity. Boone, Rawson, and Vance (2010) recommended that "schools and teachers acknowledge and explore the varied social, cultural, and ethnic backgrounds that boys bring with them to the literacy classroom, paying particular attention to the ways that constructions of masculinity influence boys' behavior and learning in literacy" (37).

Shain (2012) conducted research regarding effective literacy instruction. Research findings revealed that when teachers were supportive of students' sense of competence and self-worth, those students were more willing to believe their teachers cared about who they were as individuals, were concerned about their well-being, and genuinely wanted them to be successful learners. These ideas are important when considering ways to help boys develop into successful readers and writers. Shain found that boys are more successful in school when their teachers (a) are familiar with the text; (b) engage the reader in significant, high-interest material; (c) provide differentiated instruction that is research based and supports literacy advancement; (d) allow students to converse with each other to enhance collaboration; (e) foster an environment that is nurturing and encouraging, allowing students to be supported; (f) are adaptive to student learning needs; (g) provide flexibility within the learning environment; (h) create a culture of respect; and (i) demonstrate an understanding that all boys are different.

Maintaining Success

Jenkins (2009) contended that African American males experienced failure at every level (i.e., socially, academically, and economically) as a result of persistent biases and racial stigmatization. The author conducted a study to explore those factors that would most support increasing male readers' achievement. Findings and conclusions from the study were intended to be used to make recommendations to educators based on a longitudinal study of an African American male student in sixth grade. The student came from a divorced family of professionals and had attended the same elementary school and middle school since third grade. In kindergarten, he received speech therapy, and he repeated first grade because of low reading achievement. In grade three, he was referred for special education testing. During the study, the student put in a great deal of hard work to successfully make it to grade six. He still found reading very boring, however, and often lacked interest in the material he had to read. As a result, he read below grade level.

Jenkins (2009) suggested five recommendations to improve school literacy practices for students that may also be transferable to other students. Two are emphasized here. The first is to enable students to build on their past successes. Sadly, in the study Jenkins conducted, the student participant did not have much success. However, by allowing him to remain with effective classroom teachers for two or more years, he then would better understand and possibly adapt to instruction. The second is to help students connect their book readings to their world. A good book selection helps boys tap into their special interests, choose entertaining reading materials, address their unique questions about the world, and find more information that facilitates their participation in various activities (Jenkins 2009; Prager 2011).

No Child Left Behind legislation required all schools to meet an absolute level of performance in reading and mathematics that could be applied uniformly to all subgroups of students within a school (Dee and Jacob 2011). The law described performance in terms of annual measurable objectives, indicating the minimum percentage of students who must meet the proficiency level of performance on reading and mathematics assessments. It defined subgroups as economically disadvantaged students, students from major racial and ethnic groups, students with disabilities, and those with limited English proficiency. Moreover, the legislation required 95 percent of students overall and 95 percent of each subgroup of students within a school to take the standardized reading and mathematics tests (Dee and Jacob 2011; Research and Training Center on Independent Living 2008).

The accountability requirements of the No Child Left Behind legislation place high-poverty schools and racially diverse schools at a disadvantage because they rely on mean proficiency scores and require all subgroups to meet the same goals for accountability. School-level data from Virginia and California illustrated differences using mean proficiency scores and from rules that require students in racially diverse schools to meet multiple performance targets. Student-achievement data from six states were used to highlight differences in the demographic characteristics of schools identified as needing improvement and schools meeting the federal requirements for adequate yearly progress. Various researchers suggest alternatives for the design of accountability systems that include using multiple measures of student achievement, factoring in student improvement on achievement tests in reading and mathematics, and incorporating state accountability ratings of school performance (Dee and Jacob 2011).

To show how high-poverty schools perform under a system based on mean proficiency and value-added measures, Rawson and Hughes-Hassell (2012) analyzed student-achievement scores from three national data sets and public schools in Washington, DC. Spanning the elementary, middle, and high school grades, these analyses highlighted large differences in the cognitive skills and background characteristics of students enrolled in high-poverty and low-poverty schools. Rawson and Hughes-Hassell noted that simulations or accountability systems based on mean proficiency levels are systematically biased against high-poverty schools, and the "tendency of mean proficiency to disproportionately target high-poverty schools as failing to appear to result primarily from selection bias" (26). Despite these initial differences in mean test score levels, high-poverty schools generated annual learning gains that were similar on average to those of low-poverty schools. Nonetheless, an accountability system based on mean proficiency measures would treat many high-poverty schools as failing, even though their students' achievement test scores improved at a rate equal to those in low-poverty schools.

Under the No Child Left Behind legislation, mean proficiency levels are also used to determine the academic progress of different subgroups of students within a given school. Research by Ehren and Swanborn (2012) suggests that subgroup accountability policies have ambiguous benefits and clear costs for minority students and their schools. Kane and Staiger (2012) found little evidence that subgroup accountability rules in California and Texas improve minority student achievement. Moreover, subgroup policies in both states produced high failure rates in schools with a large percentage of African American and Latino students.

The research of Kane and Staiger (2012) has two direct implications for the policy of adequate yearly progress. First, because African American and Latino students have lower average test scores than Caucasian and Asian students, schools with either an African American or a Latino subgroup have a higher probability of failing to meet the requirements for adequate yearly progress. Second, because African American and Latino students often belong to other subgroup categories defined by No Child Left Behind, including subgroups for economically disadvantaged students and students with limited English proficiency, schools with a minority subgroup were required to meet multiple targets, which further increased the chances of failing to make adequate yearly progress.

Shortcomings and Pitfalls of Prior Research

A review of research suggests that education professionals need to take an honest position concerning the literacy development of African American adolescent males. Neither effective reading strategies nor comprehensive literacy reform efforts will close the achievement gap in a race-based and class-based society unless meaningful texts are at the curriculum's core. The curriculum represents a risk factor as well as the educational environment overall. The schooling environments of African American males are very different from their home environments, and how these students negotiate within these environments is central to their success (Au 2011).

Scholars have also investigated the effects of differences among Caucasian and African American students in their socioeconomic status, family structures, neighborhood characteristics, and the quality of their schools. A considerable amount of research suggests that socioeconomic factors, such as household income, nutrition, and self-esteem, are all significant elements that have an impact on the academic achievement of African American males. There is virtually no empirical evidence of proven practices and programs that significantly improve the reading achievement of a high percentage of African American male adolescents who enter urban high schools as struggling readers (Duke et al. 2011).

Conducting new high-quality research for improving the quality and effectiveness of educating African American males is an important issue that requires the attention of researchers. In addition, data and evidence are lacking in the following areas:

1. Data that show when warning signs are present (Children's Defense Fund 2011)
2. Evidence that addresses low-income African American boys' educational and developmental challenges by creating high-quality early-childhood education and services for children from birth to eight years old (Nyhan 2011)
3. Evidence and research that incorporate developmentally appropriate assessment processes, providing strong professional development for teachers, offering leadership development for principals, and supporting a dual-generation strategy to ensure parent and family engagement (Blair 2011)

Summary

Improving reading achievement and enhancing reading skills among African American students must remain a top priority for reading researchers. In this literature review, the writer highlighted promising areas of research to assist in examining African American high school males' reading achievement. This dissertation researcher sought to find new ways to address problems that keep the adolescent African American male population from succeeding educationally. Although a plethora of research addresses this dilemma, the major implication is to find the link between improving African American male student reading and closing the reading achievement gap by focusing on (a) teachers' efforts to stock classroom libraries with ethnically diverse books (i.e., culturally relevant literature), (b) the types of reading activities students enjoy (i.e., use of cultural material), and (c) the personal literacy behaviors of parents and the strategies they use to motivate their sons to read (i.e., parent levels of participation).

Synthesis of the Findings

Findings from the research indicate that the achievement gap remains a focus of educators, policy makers, researchers, and writers. A review of the existing literature has provided suggested strategies that could impact and improve achievement for African American males. The strategies are interrelated and encompass elements that involve in-school advocates, the importance of parental involvement, culturally responsive instruction, highly qualified teachers trained in ethnic minority and racial diversity who view all students with the potential to succeed, and schools with adequate resources and good leadership support. For the achievement gap to be effectively addressed, a comprehensive approach must be taken that incorporates individual student factors as well as all other elements that impact student achievement.

Furthermore, the literature establishes that many students from ethnic minority and nonminority backgrounds share increased challenges in their daily lives because of today's demographic trends, as indicated in many surveys, Gallup polls, and reports of the Carnegie Commission of New York. These challenges include (a) a 55 percent to 65 percent divorce rate; (b) a changing family structure involving married, remarried, and single parents, who are devoting substantial time and energy to their careers; (c) a decrease in adult supervision after school, which has resulted in more adolescents experimenting with gangs, sex, drugs, and alcohol; (d) an increase in family problems, conflicts with friends, depression, difficulties with male-female relationships, and feelings of worthlessness (these have led to a rise in the percentage of teenagers who have attempted suicide or considered suicide); and (e) an increase in the number of hours each week that elementary school children watch television (Wright 2008). Although this potentially toxic mix is detrimental to most children's emotional and intellectual development, it tends to have a greater impact on African American students. For example, 49 percent of African American children live in households with only their mothers compared with 25 percent of Hispanic children and 17 percent of Caucasian children (Noguera 2012). The economic, emotional, and intellectual pressures imposed on African American students are obvious.

To ameliorate some of this stress and help improve the academic outcomes of African American students, educators should demonstrate genuine caring as they act in specific ways to enhance achievement. Success across the curriculum is predicated on good relationships and effective literacy learning (Allington and Gabriel 2012; Division for Early Childhood 2015; Farver, Yiyuan, and Eppe 2006; Gillanders, McKinney, and Ritchie 2012). This research was intended to support this direction. Teachers and administrators should consider these and other suggestions from the professional literature and practical experience as they work in deliberate ways to improve their teaching and learning environment.

Research Questions

The following research questions were established to guide this applied dissertation:

1. Is there a statistically significant correlation between parental involvement, as measured by the parent survey, and reading achievement on the Texas Assessment of Knowledge and Skills (TAKS)?

2. Is there a statistically significant correlation between culturally responsive teacher instructional practices, as measured by the teacher checklist, and TAKS reading achievement?

Chapter 3

METHODOLOGY

Introduction

The purpose of this chapter is to highlight the methodology used to conduct the study. A quantitative, correlational design was used to examine the relationship between the reading achievement of African American males, particularly in high school settings, and specific factors that may support this achievement. Specifically, the relationships of reading achievement to the inclusion of culturally relevant reading materials, parental involvement, and culturally responsive instructional practices were considered. Recent studies, as indicated in the review of literature, led to the two research questions to examine whether supportive learning environments are correlated with higher reading achievement for African American males (Allington and Gabriel 2012; Brown 2009; Epstein 2005). The following research questions were established to guide this applied dissertation:

1. Is there a statistically significant correlation between parental involvement, as measured by the parent survey, and reading achievement on the TAKS?
2. Is there a statistically significant correlation between culturally responsive teacher instructional practices, as measured by the teacher checklist, and TAKS reading achievement?

Participants

This quantitative correlational study took place at an urban high school on the East Coast that has been recognized for three consecutive years for having a large percentage of African American males who did not meet state standards on the reading portion of the FCAT. The researcher had background knowledge of populating data in her existing position as a reading teacher for at-risk students in reading-comprehension skills. The FACT defined these skills as level one and level two. As a result, 575 students, or 50 percent of the total student population, were reading below standards, and African American males made up 30 percent of this demographic. The target population for this study involved 227 African American males in the eleventh and twelfth grades combined. All 227 students were invited to participate. The students ranged in age from seventeen to nineteen years old. The racial composition of the sample included 100 percent of African American males. Most of the males came from lower-income families, as estimated by the percentage of males receiving free and reduced-price lunches (94.5 percent). This school also qualified for Title I compensatory education funds. Seven teachers taught in the intensive reading program. There were four African American females, one Caucasian female, one Caucasian male, and one Asian male.

Instruments

The TAKS. Students in grades eleven and twelve completed the ninth-grade TAKS in English-language arts (Texas Education Agency 2009). The instrument contains twenty-eight multiple-choice questions, and students were given a three-hour testing window. Monitoring of the assessment was the overall responsibility of the researcher. Classroom teachers were provided the data once the information was analyzed along with strategies to assist classroom instruction specifically focusing on the increase of comprehension. Although the original TAKS consisted of twenty-eight multiple-choice questions and three short-answer responses, students were not required to complete the short-answer questions, since deleting them did not affect a student's raw score. According to Creswell (2013), adapting an existing instrument has pros and cons. One very important factor is that the previous validity and reliability of an instrument no longer apply. The pro of using only a portion of the existing instrument lessens completion time and thus increases response rate (Creswell 2013).

The parent survey. The survey for parents of students in prekindergarten through grade twelve, developed by the Harvard Graduate School of Education (Schueler 2013), was used to assess parents in learning more about their thoughts, feelings, and attitudes toward their child's school. This survey also provided the researcher with an understanding of the parents' views on student academic success as well as gave meaning to parents' attitudes and knowledge about the school setting in which their child was a part. The survey does not provide a specific diagnosis for parental disengagement; rather, it has been proven reliable for developing a greater understanding of the relationship between parent involvement and student success.

The survey was developed through a rigorous process conducted by a team of researchers at the Harvard Graduate School of Education. The team reviewed the relevant research literature for each scale, conducted interviews with diverse groups of parents, used current best practices in survey design to create questions that formed scales, had a panel of experts review each scale, and conducted a think-out-loud procedure to make sure parents understood items as intended. The survey is designed to conduct a needs assessment, measure change over time, and evaluate an intervention in a prekindergarten-through-grade-twelve school or organization.

Scales that can be measured include family support, child behaviors, the school's fit for the child, parent self-efficacy, family engagement, barriers to engagement, school climate, and roles and responsibilities, with one summary score that indicates parent involvement. The survey offers easy-to-understand results that can help schools and organizations to understand how family involvement can be improved. According to the Education Trust, the use of data is a powerful tool to help schools raise achievement and erase gaps among different groups. This guide is designed to help parents and community members better understand and use the data to focus their efforts on changing their schools for the better.

The teacher checklist of cultural beliefs and practices. The teacher checklist of cultural beliefs and practices, developed by the Wisconsin Department of Public Instruction (2007), is important for understanding and improving educational processes. This checklist is closely linked to teachers' strategies for coping with challenges in their daily professional lives and to their general well-being, as well as how they shape students' learning environments and influence student motivation and achievement. Good instruction, of course, is not determined simply by the teacher's background, beliefs, and attitudes; it should also be responsive to students' needs and various student, classroom, and school background factors. This checklist looks at whether teaching practices adapt to students' social and language backgrounds, grade levels, and achievement levels. The results of this checklist provide the researcher with several conclusions as they pertain to teachers' beliefs, practices, and attitudes, which all have proven to be relevant to the improvement and effectiveness of schools.

The Wisconsin Department of Public Instruction (2007) designed the teacher checklist of cultural beliefs and practices as a means for teachers not only to examine their classroom practices but also to rate school-wide culturally responsive practices. The checklist has eighteen questions that include the topics of home, student, school, and teacher. All these topics measure the home environment for reading, student performance, and teacher preparation and experience. The checklist was chosen for this research as a means to measure whether the instructional needs of individual pupils were being met and hopefully to help inform and monitor developments in the curriculum and improve learning and teaching in reading among African American male students.

The original teacher checklist was designed to address the disproportionate placement of minority students in special education and remedial tracks (Wisconsin Department of Public Instruction 2007). The revised checklist used for this study went beyond questions asked of teachers about the range of options they used to monitor pupils' progress in the classroom and moved pointedly to the area of reading instruction. Furthermore, the adapted checklist focused more on individual teacher practices as opposed to school-wide practices that support or inhibit minority student success (Wisconsin Department of Public Instruction 2007).

According to data the hosting agencies in Wisconsin gathered, results from the survey yielded positive feedback, including the following:

1. It was useful in helping staff articulate professional development needs and school improvement goals.
2. It led to deeper discussions about students of color and more patience in prereferral interventions.
3. It led to better documentation of pre-referral interventions and eligibility determination discussions.
4. It caused staff to look beyond student deficits and focus more on the environmental context (Wisconsin Department of Public Instruction 2007).

The teacher checklist helps to identify resources as well as improve reading performance among teachers by encouraging them to reflect on their cultural responsiveness to student instruction. Although this survey was originally intended for school-wide and team-based reflections, the checklist was modified to adapt to this quantitative study. The questions were adjusted by making them specific to individual teaching practices that promote or discourage cultural awareness in the classroom.

Procedures

Following the approval from the Institutional Review Board at Nova Southeastern University and the research and evaluation department in the Duval County Public Schools, students were given consent forms at school to take home to their parents. Parents were asked to return the signed consent forms, permitting their children to participate in the survey. Written assent was attained from all participant students before the survey's completion. Written consent was obtained from the seven teachers who participated in the study. The TAKS was administered to students following the completion of the informed consent and written assent forms. Approval was sought through personal communication with the Texas Education Agency followed by written communication. Following university institutional review board approval, the following schedule was used:

1. Weeks one to three: The researcher solicited involvement from targeted participants. During the first three weeks of the study, the researcher spoke with the potential teacher participants and provided them with information about the study. The researcher answered any questions and provided the teachers with an opportunity to review the documents needed for the study. Also, during this week, the researcher made a presentation to potential students and parents, informing them of the need for this study. The researcher was available to answer any questions. As for the students and parents, they also had the opportunity to review the consent forms before agreeing to participate in the study.

2. Weeks four to seven: The researcher obtained informed consent from participants. The researcher collected the informed consent forms and reviewed them to ensure accuracy. The researcher also provided participants with a timeline for the completion of the TAKS student assessment, the parent survey, and the teacher checklist. During the fourth week, teachers were provided with the teacher checklist, and the researcher administered the initial TAKS to students. The researcher planned three weeks for administering parent, student, and teacher instruments. This provided a week to collect data from each group of participants, and if participants were absent or unavailable, this provided an opportunity for makeups, if needed. The cultural checklists were given to teachers at the start of the week. Teachers had a week to complete the teacher checklist and return it to the researcher via school mail or in person during a specific pickup date and time within the week. The researcher came to the school before approval and met with participants during the first period of the school day to administer the TAKS to students. After the teacher checklist

had been administered, the students were also given the TAKS assessment, which addressed both research questions.

3. Weeks eight to eleven: The researcher analyzed the data gathered from the parent survey and teacher checklist.

Design. Correlational research has played an important role in the history of educational and psychological research (Creswell 2013). For this study, correlational research was determined to be the design structure best suited for investigating the relationships between the reading achievement of African American males and various supportive factors. Correlational research has had and will continue to have an important role in quantitative research in terms of exploring the nature of the relationships among a collection of variables. The variables in this study include the influences that may impact the educational success of African American males. These influences include parent involvement and culturally responsive instructional practices. This researcher sought to correlate these variables with the reading achievement of African American males. It was hypothesized that students who had greater levels of parental involvement and teachers who used more culturally relevant instructional practices would have a greater level of academic success.

Data analysis. The data were analyzed using Microsoft Excel spreadsheet software used for basic statistical analysis and generating graphic summaries. The research questions were answered using correlations because they were relationship questions. The steps used to analyze the data were as follows:

1. Input data into an Excel document to calculate a correlation.
2. Conduct a Pearson product-moment correlation coefficient to measure the strength and association between variables.
3. Use visuals such as histograms, box plots, and frequency tables as necessary to show representations of the data.

Lunenburg's (2011) decision chart provided the guide for organizing and summarizing the data collected in the survey conducted for this study. A descriptive statistical analysis was performed on the data collected for this study. Once data collection was completed and organized, the next step was to generate frequency tables, histograms, and box plots to see the characteristics of the data sets. The frequency tables helped to organize and summarize the data collected. The histograms and box plots provided a graphical summary of the nature of the data sets (Lunenburg 2011). Using histograms and box plots provides a visual interpretation of how the data are distributed as well as a method for visualizing any unusual characteristics (Creswell 2013).

Chapter 4

RESULTS

Introduction

The study's purpose was to examine the relationship between the reading achievement of African American males, particularly in high school settings, and specific factors that may support this achievement. Specifically, the relationship of reading achievement to parental involvement and culturally responsive instructional practices was considered. Preliminary data analyses were conducted and indicated that the Pearson correlation in reading achievement between grades eleven and twelve (i.e., Time 1 and Time 2) was .06, $p > .10$, based on a sample size of 227. This correlation was not significant. The relationship between the two variables was followed up by an examination of a scatterplot to see whether the low correlation was due to outliers or some other unexpected finding (see Appendix A). The scatterplot does not suggest any major outliers were present. However, it would appear that the upper left-hand area shows a lot of data for participants who scored very well at pretest yet very low at posttest. It was observed that several of the students did not appear to be motivated to try to do well at posttest, whereas some of these students were motivated at pretest.

All students who scored lower at posttest were removed to see whether this unusually low correlation might be due to poor student motivation at posttest. This resulted in the removal of eighty-five of these shutdown students. The Pearson correlation was recalculated and found to be .488,

$p < .001$. This correlation was obviously much higher than when the shutdown students were in the data, which suggests that the results may have been biased by a lack of student motivation at posttest. Therefore, all subsequent analyses were presented both with the full data set of 227 and the reduced dataset of 142. The breakdown of students in grades eleven and twelve is presented in Table 1. The descriptive statistics for performance on the TAKS at Time 1 and Time 2 are presented in Table 2.

Table 1

Sample Size at Both Time Periods

Item	Full data set	Reduced data set
11	159	90
12	68	52
Total	227	142

Table 2

Descriptive Statistics for Performance on Assessment

	Full data set		Reduced data set	
Item	Mean	*SD*	Mean	*SD*
Time 1	55.20	23.45	46.07	21.48
Time 2	59.35	24.51	70.03	21.90

When the data was examined further, it was determined whether there was a significant relationship between the time of assessment and reading performance for students in the reduced dataset. There should be statistically significant differences in mean reading scores if students' reading improved between Time 1 and Time 2. A repeated-measures analysis of variance was conducted to examine this possibility. The mean difference between Time 1 and Time 2 of 23.96 points on the TAKS was statistically significant, $F(1,141) = 165.02$, $p < .001$. The raw size of this effect of over twenty points is a very large difference, which indicates that the students substantially improved in reading. It is important to note that this impressive improvement was not found in the full dataset. In fact, there were no statistically significant differences in reading between periods when the shutdown students were included in the dataset (i.e., the p value was greater than .10). This suggests that one reason for the lack of improvement in reading in this population seems to be that many students do worse on reading tests when tested a second time presumably due to shutting down from lack of motivation.

Findings for Research Question One

Is there a statistically significant correlation between parental involvement, as measured by the parent survey, and reading achievement on the TAKS? To examine this research question, all parent survey items were summed up to create a composite variable that represented parental involvement. This composite variable had a mean and standard deviation of 49.20 and 17.47, respectively. Using the full dataset, the Pearson correlations between total parental involvement score and reading at pretest and posttest periods were -.038 and .021 based on a sample size of 227. Using the reduced dataset, the Pearson correlations between total parental involvement score and reading at pretest and posttest periods were -.025 and .030 based on a sample size of 142.

All correlations were trivial in size and not statistically significant. These results cannot be attributed to student shutdown at posttest, since they were obtained with the reduced dataset. Thus, no evidence indicated that parental involvement affected students' reading skills. A subsequent analysis was done to see whether each of the individual items from the parental involvement survey was related to reading skills. No significant correlations were found between reading and any of the individual parental survey items, which was consistent with the findings using the composite variable (see Appendix B).

Findings for Research Question Two

Is there a statistically significant correlation between culturally responsive teacher instructional practices, as measured by the teacher checklist, and TAKS reading achievement? To examine this research question, all teacher checklist items were summed up to create a composite variable that represented teachers' use of culturally relevant material in their classrooms. This composite variable had a mean of 47.69 and a standard deviation of 20.25. When one used the full dataset and data that were not missing, the Pearson correlations between total culturally relevant material and reading at pretest and posttest periods were .122 and .034 based on a sample size of 227.

When one used the reduced dataset and data that were not missing, the Pearson correlations between total culturally relevant material and reading at pretest and posttest periods were .159 and .097 based on a sample size of 142. The significant value for the first correlation was $p = .059$, which just exceeded the significance of .05. Thus, there was very weak to nonexistent evidence in this study that culturally relevant material in the classroom affected students' reading skills. A subsequent analysis was done to see whether each of the individual items from the teacher checklist pertaining to culturally relevant practices in the classroom was related to reading skills.

There were significant correlations between some of the individual items on the classroom teacher checklist and TAKS reading scores (see Appendix C). The posttest for the full data set included all 227 students in the study. As indicated in the full data set, there were significant correlations on items three, four, seven, and ten, which examined attitudes and relationships pertaining to the support of students. The reduced data set provided evidence for significant correlations on items three, four, five, ten, and eighteen. Thus, both data sets consistently showed evidence for correlations between the classroom teacher checklist for instructional practices and three items that measured the support of students.

Chapter 5

DISCUSSION

Introduction

In this study, the researcher analyzed the relationship between the reading achievements of African American males, particularly in high school settings, and both parental involvement and culturally responsive instructional practices. The expected outcome was to find correlations between African American parental involvement and reading achievement. Also, it was expected that culturally responsive teacher instructional practices would correlate with student reading achievement.

Summary and Interpretation of the Findings

This study was designed to answer two research questions. The first research question asked the following: Is there a statistically significant correlation between parental involvement, as measured by the parent survey, and reading achievement on the TAKS? The answer to the first research question was that no significant correlation emerged between the measure of parent involvement and student reading achievement. The second research question asked the following: Is there a statistically significant correlation between culturally responsive teacher instructional practices, as measured by the teacher checklist, and TAKS reading achievement? Five significant correlations were found between individual items on the teacher checklist and TAKS reading achievement.

Specifically, significant correlations were found between reading achievement and (a) an attitude that all students are our students, (b) teacher collaboration to support all students, (c) the availability of differentiated reading interventions, (d) the consideration of a student's family situation by the instructional team, and (e) the explicit instruction of learning strategies. Although these correlations were significant, it should be stressed that the associations between these variables and reading achievement were rather small, with correlations ranging between only .13 to .19 in magnitude. Also, the remaining correlations reported in this study were so small that they did not pass the conventional levels of statistical significance.

Context and Implications of the Findings

The following paragraphs provide a discussion of the context and implications of the findings as related to research questions one and two. Research question one related to the connection between parent involvement and reading achievement. Research question two related to the connection between culturally responsive instructional practices and reading achievement.

Research Question One. The current findings suggesting the lack of a relationship between parental involvement and student achievement may be due to a rather uniform lack of parental involvement in the current sample. A review of research conducted on parental involvement and African American males shows that African American parents are less involved in their child's academic lives than parents from other racial or ethnic groups (Neblett et al. 2009). By examining some of the negative experiences of African American students within academic settings, research has shown that there are various ways in which race is related to academic achievement. However, the current study suggests that finding empirical evidence for this relationship can be a challenge. Current findings suggest that perhaps the aspects of parent involvement studied here were not important. However, that does not mean that there are no other types of parental inputs that might be important. More work is needed so that parental involvement in the African American community may be accurately represented in the current literature.

The lack of strong correlations found here does suggest the need to further investigate parental involvement instead of just assuming that parents are not important contributors to student success. Despite the importance of parental involvement, because of a widely believed myth that African American parents do not care about their children's education, the relationship between African American parents and public school educators has historically been strained (Noguera 2008). However, researchers have repeatedly insisted that this assumption is wrong (Neblett et al. 2009). Noguera (2012) emphasized that most African American parents are extremely concerned about their children's education. According to the author, this fact remains true, even for parents of low achievers. Although the parents of low achievers are often overwhelmed by life's stressors, they still care about their children's education. Therefore, one way for educators to improve the reading skills and test scores of African American students is to make parents their allies instead of viewing them as adversaries (Noguera 2012). This might result in stronger relationships between parent involvement and student achievement.

The first step in making African American parents allies requires educators to get rid of their negative beliefs about African American parents. This means educators must eradicate their negative stereotypes about African Americans. The research indicates that many teachers do not believe that most African American parents are concerned about their children's education (Hayes 2011; Noguera 2008). Just as educators must examine and address their deficient mindsets about African American students through ongoing, intensive personal and professional development work, they must do the same regarding their negative beliefs about African American parents. Unfortunately, the findings in this study did not find contradictory evidence against this false assumption. Future work is needed to find the evidence required to change teacher biases concerning African American parents' interest in their child's education.

Although we know that parents are integral to the lives of all young children, there is no one-size-fits-all approach to effectively engaging them in programs and services designed to support the positive development of children and healthy family functioning. As research continues to examine how best to engage African American parents in particular, the influence of cultural beliefs about parenting and issues of cultural relevance should remain at the forefront. There is still much to learn, but we do know that parents across cultures want the best for their children. The task at hand is to help parents meet their parenting goals in ways that are respectful and supportive, and that reflect the growing diversity of US families.

Research Question Two. Findings concerning the teacher survey suggest some interesting relationships between culturally responsive instructional practices and reading achievement. Cultural responsiveness begins when a teacher recognizes the cultural capital and tools students of color bring to the classroom. For example, a reading teacher who was not having much success with her tenth-grade students learning vocabulary assigned a word list. Instead of continuing to have students look up the words in the dictionary, the teacher redesigned the word study using some combination of the cultural tools familiar to students (Li 2011).

The first two findings of this study were related to a school-wide team approach, involving an attitude that all students are our students and collaboration among all teachers and staff to support students. Duke et al. (2011) identified the essential elements of fostering and teaching reading comprehension. They included building disciplinary knowledge, providing exposure to a volume and range of texts, and offering motivating texts and contexts for reading. Other essential elements included teaching strategies for comprehending, teaching text structures, engaging students in discussion, building vocabulary and language knowledge, and integrating reading.

The strong research base for teaching reading should benefit all students as they progress through schools, including African American male youth in schools that are characteristically urban. Other moderating influences on the reading achievement of African American male youth include cultural attitudes; academic climate; racial demographics of schools; the relationship between neighborhood quality and schooling (Blair 2009, 2011; Boone, Rawson, and Vance 2010; Epstein 2005; Graham and Anderson 2008; Graves and Howes 2011; Hayes 2011); and how social processes of race, class, and gender are interwoven in literacy (Allington and Gabriel 2012; Heckman 2011a, 2011b; Mandara 2006; Noguera 2008, 2012; Tatum and Muhammad 2012).

Although many suggested frameworks have been proposed to improve the reading achievement of African American male youth in urban schools, more carefully controlled studies in schools in which African American male youth struggle with reading are needed. There is a need to conduct large-scale research studies in school districts that are characteristically urban and look at the literacy development of African American male youth. Second, there is a need to include the voices of African American male youth in literacy research, particularly the voices of young males who have moved beyond the primary grades. Third, more attention needs to be given to text types, characteristics of texts, and the role of texts in advancing the literacy development of African American male youth. There is ample historical precedent of the roles of text in shaping the lives of African American males in the United States (Holloway 2006; Tatum and Muhammad 2012).

The third significant finding in this study was related to the availability of differentiated reading instruction. This finding is consistent with the previous studies in this area. Duke et al. (2011) identified the essential elements of fostering and teaching reading comprehension. They included building disciplinary knowledge, providing exposure to a volume and range of texts, and offering motivating texts and contexts for reading. Other essential elements included teaching strategies for comprehending, teaching text structures, engaging students in discussion, building vocabulary and language knowledge, integrating reading and writing, observing and assessing students, and differentiating instruction.

One implication is that the disproportionate representation of culturally and linguistically diverse students in high-incidence special education programs (e.g., mental retardation, learning disabilities, and emotional disturbance) has been a concern for more than thirty years (Noguera 2008). Extensive research suggests many factors are at play in the disproportionate representation of minority students in special education, including teachers' lack of knowledge about culturally and linguistically diverse children (Waters, Cross, and Shaw 2010) and their propensity to label the behavior of these students as negative and inappropriate (Noguera 2008). Noguera (2008) recommended the creation of a culturally responsive education system grounded in the belief that all culturally and linguistically diverse students can excel in school when their culture, language, heritage, and experiences are valued and used to facilitate their learning and development and they are provided access to high-quality teachers, programs, and resources.

Many students of color have an understanding of, and some have internalized, negative images of their race (Gay 2000). These negative images, promoted by the larger society, affect how they perform in school (Noguera 2003). A culturally responsive pedagogy allows for the discussion of difficult topics, such as racism, discrimination, and prejudice. It also offers students of all ages the opportunity to engage in meaningful discussion that enhances learning. The principles of differentiated instruction lend themselves to the culturally responsive pedagogical approach because they create opportunities for a myriad of investigations into one lesson or topic at the same time. With differentiated instruction, students of color can explore a topic through a teaching approach that best meets their learning styles while examining the values, beliefs, and ideas that shape their experiences.

The fourth significant finding of this study was related to the instructional team's understanding of the student's home situation. This finding is consistent with previous findings in this area. In 2017, the gap showed up in the results of California's annual standardized test, called the California Assessment of Student Performance and Progress (California Department of Education 2017). About two-thirds of students from low-income families did not meet grade-level standards in English-language arts and literacy. For students who did not come from low-income families, the ratio was flipped, since about two-thirds of those students met grade-level standards. The relationship to poverty is amplified at the extremes. For example, about one-third of students from a family not living in poverty scored in the range of exceeding standards. However, only one in ten students from a low-income family did so (California Department of Education 2017).

In 2011, Stanford sociologist Sean F. Reardon compiled data to quantify the achievement gap between children from rich families and children from poor families. The author concluded that the test score differences associated with poverty were considerably greater than those associated with race. Reardon also found that the gaps were growing. Given the research regarding the underachievement of African Americans in the area of reading, it is clear that more studies are needed that examine the direct and unique effects of reading achievement for high school students (Allington and Gabriel 2012; Noguera 2012; Rowley 2000). Although several scholarly works have been produced to better understand the impact of critical factors on the reading achievement of African American students in the early grades, few studies exist that focus on African American high school students (Flowers 2003; Lee and Bowen 2006). Thus, additional research is needed to highlight some of the issues that affect the reading achievement of African American students at the high school level to inform educational reform and curriculum-development activities.

Finally, the fifth significant finding was related to the explicit instruction of learning strategies. Strong teacher content knowledge and instructional skills are also linked to increased student achievement (Epstein 2005; Fashola 2013; Ladson-Billings 2009). Culturally relevant literacy instruction is instruction that builds a gap between the school and the students' worlds, and it is consistent with the values of the students' own culture aimed at ensuring academic learning (Au 2011). Another important principle of culturally relevant teaching involves instructional materials that use students' identities and backgrounds as a foundation for learning and thus connect their students' perspectives to the larger social context.

Some proponents of culturally relevant teaching argue that the academic achievement and school performance of students improved when curriculum and pedagogy were relevant to students' lives (Ladson-Billings 2009; Tatum 2008b). Although this is intuitively appealing, Ladson-Billings (2009) offered examples of an exemplary implementation of culturally responsive instruction for Native American peoples but offered no evidence of positive outcome results in school retention or academic achievement for African American males. More rigorous study is needed to establish this promising practice as fact.

Likewise, claims that stories with multicultural themes will motivate students to increase reading practice are not yet supported by research evidence. For example, in a study of thirty-five African American and Caucasian third-grade students in Mississippi, Holmes et al. (2010) found that, contrary to their expectations, students more often selected books with characters of different, not similar, racial backgrounds. Based on the results of their review, the authors concluded that offering books about dissimilar people may promote interracial awareness and an understanding for children of diverse cultural and socioeconomic backgrounds. In a similar vein, Harris and Lee (2006) argued that stories in direct instruction curricula are not likely to be culturally interesting or appropriate for the population in juvenile correction facilities. Yet evidence suggests that diverse students using these materials make significant progress in reading achievement (National Education Association 2011).

Limitations

As with any study, there are potential limitations that should be considered when both interpreting the present results and thinking about future research to conduct. The most obvious limitation of convenience sampling is sampling bias and that the sample is not representative of the entire population. This may be the biggest disadvantage when using a convenience sample. Because the sample is not representative of the population, the results of the study cannot speak for the entire population. This results in a low external validity of the study. According to Creswell (2013), the external validity represents the extent to which a study's results can be generalized or applied to other people or settings.

A second potential limitation is that the study was conducted in the fall and that during this time students had been in school less than ninety days. The reading measures of students were collected in the spring after state testing. There is a possibility that the correlations would have been stronger if all data had been collected toward the end of the school year. Thus, changes in student learning from fall to spring could have reduced the estimated correlations between variables. Ideally, the measurement of parent and student inputs along with reading achievement would be done during multiple times during the school year. That way teachers could use the knowledge gained in the fall to help guide instruction and communication with parents at a time when there were still enough days in the school year for teacher behaviors to make an effect on student learning.

Finally, it is important to acknowledge that, in addition to the parental involvement and teacher instructional practices explored through this study, other variables play a role in improving the reading achievement of African American male students. These are outside the scope of this study and may be investigated through future studies, such as limited resources, school funding, and extended learning opportunities during and after school.

Future Research Directions

The research studies suggested above by the stated limitations will possibly provide needed information to assist today's educators and leaders in determining how to capture the unused academic potential of many African American male students. In addition, further research using qualitative research methods will enable the researcher to learn directly from students what factors African American male students associate with academic success as well as challenges to academic success and solutions for achieving academic success. By using qualitative methods, it is possible to find out what factors seem to provide barriers to successful learning in school. As Marshall and Rossman (1999) stated, it is possible to find a natural solution to these barriers, probably without changing school policies. Instead, teachers can, for example, learn what prevents parents from assisting their child in school and offer solutions such as frequent communication and feedback for parents to use in assisting their child's learning at home. Qualitative research, as a broad strategy for learning from children and parents, can document in a more naturalistic and readily interpretable way than a brief survey what factors can help students to achieve.

REFERENCES

Aarons, D. 2010. "Diploma Rates Found to Lag for African American Males: 'Yes We Can': The 2010 Schott 50 State Report on African American Males in Public Education." *Education Week* 30 (1): 5–9.

Allington, R. L., and R. E. Gabriel. 2012. "Every Child, Every Day." *Educational Leadership* 69 (6): 10–15.

Arnold, D. H., A. Zeljo, G. L. Doctoroff, and C. Ortiz. 2008. "Parent Involvement in Preschool: Predictors and the Relation of Involvement to Preliteracy Development." *School Psychology Review* 37 (1): 74–91.

Au, K. H. 2006. *Multicultural Issues and Literacy Achievement.* Mahwah, NJ: Erlbaum.

Au, K. H. 2011. *Literacy Achievement and Diversity: Keys to Success for Students, Teachers, and Schools.* New York: Teachers College Press.

Averitt, J. 2011. "African American Male Students' Perceptions of Factors That Contribute to Their Academic Success" Unpublished PhD diss., Georgia Southern University, Statesboro.

Banks, L., and M. Oliveira. 2011. "Report to the Mayor from the Chairs." New York: Young Men's Initiative.

Blair, C. 2009. "Critical Race Theory: A Framework to Study the Early Reading Intervention Strategies of Primary Grades Teachers working with African American Male Students" PhD diss. Available from ProQuest Dissertations and Theses database. (UMI No. 3694609)

Blair, C. 2011. "Salivary Cortisol Mediates Effects of Poverty and Parenting on Executive Functions in Early Childhood." *Child Development* 82 (6): 1970–84.

Boone, J., C. Rawson, and K. Vance. 2010. "Getting It Right: Building a Bridge to Literacy for Adolescent African American Males. *School Library Monthly* 27 (2): 34–37.

Brotherson, S., and J. White. 2007. *Why Fathers Count*. Nashville: Men's Studies Press.

Brown, P. 2009. "Involving Parents in the Education of Their Children." Urbana, IL: ERIC Clearinghouse on Elementary and Early Childhood Education.

Butler, S. K., M. A. Shillingford, and M. Alexander-Snow. 2011. "African American Male Students and the Achievement Gap: Building a Successful Student/Citizen." *Inter-American Journal of Psychology* 34 (2): 177–83.

California Department of Education. 2017. *State Schools Chief Tom Torlakson Announces Results of California Assessment of Student Performance and Progress Online Tests*. Sacramento, CA: self-published.

Casserly, M., S. Lewis, C. Simon, R. Uzzell, and M. Palacios. 2012. *A Call for Change: Providing Solutions for Black Male Achievement*. Washington, DC: Council of the Great City Schools.

Center on Education Policy. 2012. *What Roles Do Parent Involvement, Family Background, and Culture Play in Student Motivation?* Washington, DC: self-published.

Children's Defense Fund. 2011. *Portrait of Inequality 2011: Black Children in America*. Washington, DC: self-published.

Coggins, P., and S. D. Campbell. 2008. "Using Cultural Competence to Close the Achievement Gap." *Journal of Pan African Studies* 2: 139–40.

Creswell, J. W. 2013. *Qualitative Inquiry: Choosing among Five Approaches*. Thousand Oaks, CA: Sage.

Crosnoe, R., C. Riegle-Crumb, K. Frank, S. Field, and C. Muller. 2010. "Peer Group Contexts of Girls' and Boys' Academic Experiences." *Child Development* 79 (1): 139–55. https://doi.org/10.1111/j.1467-8624.2007.01116.x.

Dawkins, M., J. Braddock, and A. Celaya. 2008. "Academic Engagement among African American Males Who Hold Aspirations for Athletic Careers in Professional Sports." *Challenge* 14 (2): 51–65.

Dee, T. S., and B. Jacob. 2011. "The Impact of No Child Left Behind on Student Achievement." *Journal of Policy Analysis and Management* 30: 418–19.

Division for Early Childhood. 2015. *DEC Position Statement on Responsiveness to All Children, Families, and Professionals: Integrating Cultural and Linguistic Diversity into Policy and Practice*. Washington, DC: self-published.

Douglass, F., and H. A. Baker. 1982. *Narrative of the Life of Frederick Douglass, an American Slave*. Harmondsworth, England: Penguin Books.

Duke, N., P. D. Pearson, L. Strachan, and A. K. Billman. 2011. "Essential Elements of Fostering and Teaching Reading Comprehension." In *What Research Has to Say about Reading Instruction*, edited by S. J. Samuels and A. Farstrup, 233–39. Newark, DE: International Reading Association.

Educational Testing Service. 2011. *Addressing Achievement Gaps. Positioning Young Black Boys for Educational Success*. Princeton, NJ: self-published.

Edwards, P. A. 1992. "Involving Parents in Building Reading Instruction for African American Children." *Theory into Practice* 31 (3): 350–59.

Edwards, P. A. 2004. *Children's Literacy Development: Making It Happen through School, Family, and Community Involvement*. Boston: Allyn & Bacon.

Ehren, M. C. M., and M. S. L. Swanborn. 2012. "Strategic Data Use of Schools in Accountability Systems." *School Effectiveness and School Improvement* 23 (2): 257–58.

Entwisle, D. R., and K. L. Alexander. 1988. "Factors Affecting Achievement Test Scores and Marks of Black and White First Graders." *Elementary School Journal* 88: 449–71. https://doi.org/10.1086/461550.

Epstein, J. L. 2005. "School-Initiated Family and Community Partnerships." In *This We Believe in Action: Implementing Successful Middle Level Schools*, edited by T. Erb, 77–96. Westerville, OH: National Middle School Association.

Epstein, J. L. 2008. "Improving Family and Community Involvement in Secondary Schools." *Education Digest* 73 (6): 9–12.

Epstein, J. L. 2011. "Can the Epstein Model of Parental Involvement Work in a High-Minority, High-Poverty Elementary School?" *Professional School Counseling* 5 (2): 77–87.

Esposito, J., and A. N. Swain. 2009. "Pathways to Social Justice: Urban Teachers' Uses of Culturally Relevant Pedagogy as a Conduit for Teaching for Social Justice." *Urban Education* 23 (1): 38–48.

Farver, J., X. Yiyuan, and S. Eppe. 2006. "Home Environments and Young Latino Children's School Readiness." *Childhood Research Quarterly* 21 (2): 196–212.

Fashola, O. 2013. "Evaluation of an Extended School Day Program for African American Males in the Context of Single-Gender Schooling and Schoolwide Reform: A Case for Extending the School Day for African American Males." *Peabody Journal of Education* 88: 488–517.

Florida Department of Education. 2014. *Florida High School Graduation Rates, 2014–2015*. Tallahassee, FL: self-published.

Flowers, T. A. 2003. "Exploring the Influence of Reading for Pleasure on African American High School Students' Reading Achievement." *High School Journal* 87: 58–62.

Ford, D. Y., and J. L. Moore. 2013. "Understanding and Reversing Underachievement, Low Achievement, and Achievement Gaps among High-Ability African American Males in Urban School Contexts." *Urban Review* 45 (4): 399–415.

Gantt, A., and G. Greif. 2009. "African American Single Mothers Raising Sons: Implications for Family Therapy." *Journal of Family Social Work* 12: 227–43.

Garrity, P. A. 2009. "Effective Pedagogical Practices for Teaching African American Students in a K-8 Urban Charter School." Unpublished PhD. diss., California State University, Long Beach.

Gay, G. 2010. *Culturally Responsive Teaching: Theory, Research, and Practice*. New York: Teachers College Press.

Gillanders, C., M. McKinney, and S. Ritchie. 2012. "What Kind of School Would You Like for Your Children? Exploring Minority Mothers'

Beliefs to Promote Home-School Partnerships." *Early Childhood Education Journal* 40: 285–94.

Gordon, D., D. Iwamoto, N. Ward, R. Potts, and E. Boyd. 2009. "Mentoring Urban African American Middle School Male Students: Implications for Academic Achievement." *Journal of Negro Education* 78: 277–364.

Graham, A., and K. A. Anderson. 2008. "'I Have to Be Three Steps Ahead': Academically Gifted African American Male Students in an Urban High School on the Tension between an Ethnic Identity and Academic Identity." *Urban Review* 40 (5): 472–99.

Graves, S. L., and C. Howes. 2011. "Ethnic Differences in Social-Emotional Development in Preschool: The Impact of Teacher Child Relationships and Classroom Quality. *School Psychology Quarterly* 26 (3): 202–14.

Greenleaf, C. L., and K. Hinchman. 2009. "Reimagining Our Inexperienced Adolescent Readers: From Struggling, Striving, Marginalized, and Reluctant to Thriving." *Journal of Adolescent and Adult Literacy* 53: 4–13.

Greenwood, S. J. 2011. "Culturally Responsive Pedagogy: A Study of Implementation." Unpublished PhD. diss., California State University, Long Beach.

Gregory, A., R. J. Skiba, and P. A. Noguera. 2010. "The Achievement Gap and the Discipline Gap: Two Sides of the Same Coin?" *Educational Researcher* 39 (1): 59–68. https://doi.org/10.3102/0013189X09357621.

Guest, A., and B. Schneider. 2013. "Adolescents' Extracurricular Participation in Context: The Mediating Effects of Schools, Communities, and Identity." *Sociology of Education* 76 (2): 89–109.

Guthrie, J. T., and J. Cambria. 2011. *Best Practices for Motivating Students to Read*. New York: Guilford Press.

Hale, J. E. 2001. *Learning While Black: Creating Educational Excellence for African American Children*. Baltimore: Johns Hopkins University Press.

Hall, L. A., and S. V. Piazza. 2008. "Critically Reading Texts: What Students Do and How Teachers Can Help." *Reading Teacher* 62: 32–41.

Hamilton, P. 2009. "African American Education: Have We Made Progress?" *Journal of Higher Education* 25: 19–21.

Harris, V. W., and T. R. Lee. 2006. "Using Empirically Based Methodologies to Teach Family Life Education Topics Effectively." *Journal of Teaching in Marriage and Family* 6: 121–39.

Harris, W. G., and G. W. Duhon. 1999. *The African American Perspective of Barriers to Success.* New York: Mellen Press.

Hartney, M. T., and P. Flavin. 2014. "The Political Foundations of the Black-White Education Achievement Gap." *American Politics Research* 42 (1): 3–9.

Hayes, D. 2011. "Predicting Parental Home and School Involvement in High School African American Adolescents." *High School Journal* 94: 154–66.

Heckman, J. 2011a. "The American Family in Black and White: A Post-Racial Strategy for Improving Skills to Promote Equality." *Daedalus* 140 (2): 70–89.

Heckman, J. 2011b. "The Economics of Inequality." *Education Digest* 77 (4): 4–11.

Hill, N. E., D. R. Castellino, J. E. Lansford, P. Nowlin, K. A. Dodge, and J. Bates. 2011. "Parent Academic Involvement as Related to School Behavior, Achievement, and Aspirations: Demographic Variations across Adolescence." *Child Development* 75 (6): 1491–1509.

Hill, N. E., and D. Tyson. 2009. "Parental Involvement in Middle School: A Meta-Analytic Assessment of the Strategies That Promote Achievement." *Developmental Psychology* 45 (5): 740–763. https://doi.org/10.1037/a0015362.

Hines, E., and C. Holcomb-McCoy. 2013. "Parental Characteristics, Ecological Factors, and the Academic Achievement of African American Males." *Journal of Counseling and Development* 91: 68–77.

Holloway, K. 2006. *Bookmarks: Reading in Black and White.* New Brunswick, NJ: Rutgers University Press.

Holmes, K., S. Powell, S. Holmes, and E. Witt. 2010. "Readers and Book Characters? Does Race Matter?" *Journal of Education Research* 100: 276–82. https://doi.org/10.3200 /JOER.100.5.276-282.

Holt, J. K., and M. C. Smith. 2005. "Literacy Practices among Different Ethnic Groups: The Role of Socioeconomic and Cultural Factors." *Literacy Research and Instruction* 44 (3): 1–21.

Huang, G. H., and K. L. Mason. 2008. "Motivations of Parental Involvement in Children's Learning: Voices from Urban African American Families of Preschoolers." *Multicultural Education* 15 (3): 20–27.

Hughes, R. L. 2010. "Engaging African American Males for Educational Success." *Gifted Child Today* 33 (2): 55–60.

Jenkins, S. 2009. "How to Maintain School Reading Success: Five Recommendations from a Struggling Male Reader." *Reading Teacher* 63: 159–62.

Joe, E., and J. Davis. 2009. "Parental Influence, School Readiness, and Early Academic Achievement of African American Boys." *Journal of Negro Education* 3 (19): 260–63.

Kailin, J. 2006. "Antiracist Education." *TESOL Quarterly* 40 (3): 649–651.

Kane, T. J., and D. O. Staiger. 2012. "Gathering Feedback for Teachers: Combining High-Quality Observations with Student Surveys and Achievement Gains." Seattle: Bill and Melinda Gates Foundation.

Karchmer-Klein, R., and V. H. Shinas. 2012. "Guiding Principles for Supporting New Literacies in Your Classroom." *Reading Teacher* 65: 288–89.

Kenyatta, C. P. 2012. "From Perception to Practice: How Teacher-Student Interactions Affect African American Male Achievement." *Journal of Urban Learning Teaching and Research* 8: 36–44.

Kirkland, D. E. 2011. "Listening to Echoes: Teaching Young African American Men Literacy and the Distraction of ELA Standards." *Language Arts* 88 (5): 373–80.

Korat, O. 2011. "Mothers' and Teachers' Estimations of First Graders' Literacy Level and Their Relation to the Children's Actual Performance in Different SES Groups." *Education and Treatment of Children* 34 (3): 347–71.

Kozol, J. 1991. *Savage Inequalities: Children in America's Schools.* New York: Crown.

Kunjufu, J. 2005. *Keeping African American Boys out of Special Education.* Sauk Village, IL: African American Images.

Ladson-Billings, G. 1995. "Toward a Theory of Culturally Relevant Pedagogy." *American Education Journal* 35: 465–91.

Ladson-Billings, G. 2009. *The Dreamkeepers: Successful Teachers of African American Students*. San Francisco: Jossey-Bass.

Lee, J., and N. Bowen. 2006. "Parent Involvement, Cultural Capital, and the Achievement Gap among Elementary School Children." *American Educational Research Journal* 43: 193–218.

Lewis, C., B. Butler, F. Bonner, and M. Joubert. 2010. "African American Male Discipline Patterns and School District Responses Resulting Impact on Academic Achievement: Implications for Urban Educators and Policy Makers." *Journal of African American Males In Education* 1: 7–25.

Li, G. 2011. "The Role of Culture in Literacy, Learning, and Teaching." In *Handbook of Reading Research*, edited by M. L. Kamil, P. D. Pearson, E. B. Moje, and P. P. Afflerbach, 515–38. New York: Routledge.

Logan, B. C. 2013. "The Impact of Religious Commitment and Motivation on African American Male Academic Achievement." Unpublished PhD diss., Georgia Southern University, Statesboro.

Lopez, R. 2011. "The Impact of Parental Involvement on African American Student Achievement." *Journal of Multiculturalism in Education* 7: 11–19.

Lunenburg, C. 2011. "Decision Making in Organizations." *International Journal of Management, Business, and Administration* 15: 25–27.

Mandara, J. 2006. "The Impact of Family Functioning on African American Males' Academic Achievement: A Review and Clarification of the Empirical Literature." *Teachers College Record* 108 (2): 206–23.

Marshall, C., and G. B. Rossman. 1999. *Designing Qualitative Research*. Thousand Oaks, CA: Sage.

Martin, D., M. Martin, S. S. Gibson, and J. Wilkins. 2007. "Increasing Prosocial Behavior and Academic Achievement among Adolescent African American Males." *Adolescence* 42 (168): 689–98.

McCullough, R. 2013. "The Relationship between Reader Response and Prior Knowledge on African American Students' Reading Comprehension Performance Using Multicultural Literature." *Reading Psychology* 34 (5): 397–435.

McLaughlin, M., and G. L. DeVoogd. 2014. *Critical Literacy: Enhancing Students' Comprehension of the Text*. New York: Scholastic.

Meier, D., and G. Wood. 2014. *Many Children Left Behind: How the No Child Left Behind Act Is Damaging Our Children and Our Schools*. Boston: Beacon Press.

Montero, M. 2007. "The Political Psychology of Liberation: From Politics to Ethics and Back." *Political Psychology* 28 (1): 22–23.

Morris, V. 2011. "The Street Lit Author and the Inner-City Teen Reader." *Young Adult Library Services* 10 (1): 21–24.

Mullins, D. 2010. "Linkages between Children's Behavior and Nonresident Father Involvement: A Comparison of African American, Anglo, and Latino Families." *Journal of African American Studies* 15: 1–21.

National Center for Education Statistics. 2010. *National Reading Assessment*. Washington, DC: self-published.

National Center for Education Statistics. 2011. *Condition of Education 2011*. Washington, DC: self-published.

National Center for Education Statistics. 2013. *The National Assessment of Educational Progress: Understanding Gaps*. Washington, DC: self-published.

National Center for Education Statistics. 2015. *The National Assessment of Educational Progress: Black-White Achievement Performance*. Washington, DC: self-published.

National Education Association. 2011. *Focus on Blacks: Race against Time: Educating Black Boys*. Washington, DC: self-published.

Nebbitt, V. E., M. Lombe, V. LaPoint, and D. Bryant. 2009. "Predictors and Correlates of Academic Performance among Urban African American Adolescents." *Journal of Negro Education* 78: 29–41.

Neblett, E. W., T. M. Chavous, H. X. Nguyen, and R. M. Sellers. 2009. "'Say It Loud–I'm Black and I'm Proud': Parents' Messages about Race, Racial Discrimination, and Academic Achievement in African American Boys." *Journal of Negro Education* 78: 246–59.

Neely, A. 2012. *Teaching African American Males: A Look at Instructional Methods and Cultural Differences*. Sacramento: California State University.

Nichols, J. D., and J. White. 2001. "Impact of Peer Networks on Achievement of High School Algebra Students." *Journal of Educational Research* 94: 267–73.

Noguera, P. A. 2002. "Beyond School Size: The Challenge of High School Reform." *Educational Leadership* 59 (5): 60–63.

Noguera, P. A. 2003. "The Trouble with African American Boys: The Role and Influence of Environmental and Cultural Factors on the Academic Performance of African American Males." *Urban Education* 38 (4): 431–59.

Noguera, P. A. 2008. *Creating Schools Where Race Does Not Matter: The Role and Significance of Race in the Racial Achievement Gap.* Thousand Oaks, CA: Sage.

Noguera, P. A. 2012. "Saving Black and Latino Boys." *Phi Delta Kappan* 93: 8–12.

Nyhan, P. 2011. *The Power of Pre-K-3rd: How a Small Foundation Helped Push Washington State to the Forefront of the Pre-K-3rd Movement.* New York: Foundation for Child Development.

Olukolu, R. 2013. *The Relationship of Culturally Responsive Instruction and the Reading Comprehension and Attitude of Struggling Urban Adolescent Readers.* Miami: Florida International University.

Ortiz, R. W. 2001. "Pivotal Parents: Emergent Themes and Implications on Father Involvement in Children's Early Literacy Experiences." *Reading Improvement* 38 (2): 132–44.

Piazza, S. V., and L. E. Duncan. 2012. "After-School Literacy Engagements with Struggling Readers." *Reading Writing Quarterly* 28 (3): 229–54.

Prado, L., and L. Plourde. 2011. "Increasing Reading Comprehension through the Explicit Teaching of Reading Strategies: Is There a Difference among the Genders?" *Reading Improvement* 48 (1): 32–43.

Prager, K. 2011. "Children's Defense Fund Opens Summer Program for Black Boys." *Education Daily* 44 (123): 4–8.

Raftery, J., W. Grolnick, and E. Flamm. 2012. "Families as Facilitators of Student Engagement: Toward a Home-School Partnership Model." In *Handbook of Research on Student Engagement*, edited by S. Christenson, A. Reschly, and C. Wylie, 343–64. New York: Springer.

Rawson, C., and S. Hughes-Hassell. 2012. "Rethinking the Texts We Use in Literacy Instruction with Adolescent African American Males." *ALAN Review* 39 (3): 21–29.

Reardon, S. F. 2011. "The Widening Academic Achievement Gap between the Rich and the Poor: New Evidence and Possible Explanations." In *Whither Opportunity? Rising Inequality and the Uncertain Life Chances of Low-Income Children*, edited by R. Murnane and G. Duncan, 111–68. New York: Russell Sage Foundation Press.

Research and Training Center on Independent Living. 2008. *Guidelines for Reporting and Writing about People with Disabilities*. Lawrence, KS: self-published.

Roberts, J., J. Jurgens, and M. Burchinal. 2005. "The Role of Home Literacy Practices in Preschool Children's Language and Emergent Literacy Skills." *Journal of Speech, Language, and Hearing Research* 48: 345–59.

Roney, M. 2011. "A Most Critical Need: Why All Middle Grades Educators Should Be Teachers of Reading." *North Carolina Middle School Journal* 33: 123–25.

Rowley, S. J. 2000. "Profiles of African American College Students' Educational Utility and Performance: A Cluster Analysis." *Journal of Black Psychology* 26: 3–26. https://doi.org/10.1177/009579840 0026001001.

Schueler, B. 2013. *A New Tool for Understanding Family-School Relationships: The Harvard Graduate School of Education PreK-12 Parent Survey*. Cambridge, MA: Harvard Family Research Project.

Senechal, M., and L. Young. 2008. "The Effect of Family Literacy Interventions on Children's Acquisition of Reading from Kindergarten to Grade 3: A Meta-Analytic Review." *Review of Educational Research* 78 (8): 880–907. https://doi.org/10.3102/0034.6543 .08320319.

Shain, F. 2012. "'Getting on' rather than 'getting by': Ethnicity, class, and 'success against the odds.'" *British Journal of Sociology of Education* 33: 153–55.

Sheldon, S. 2009. *Review of Research: Family and Community Involvement in Reading*. Baltimore: Johns Hopkins University.

Shor, I. 2009. "What Is Critical Literacy?" In *The Critical Pedagogy Reader*, edited by A. Darder, M. P. Baltodano, and R. D. Torres, 282–97. New York: Routledge.

Sleeter, C. E., and C. A. Grant. 2003. *Making Choices for Multicultural Education: Five Approaches to Race, Class, and Gender*. New York: Wiley.

Somers, C. L., D. Owens, and M. Piliawsky. 2008. "Individual and Social Factors Related to Urban African American Adolescents' School Performance." *High School Journal* 91: 1–11.

Spellings, M. 2012. "The Jobs Are There, the Education Is Not." *USA Today*, September 20, 2012.

Stevans, L. 2009. "The Relationship among African American Male Earnings, Employment, Incarceration, and Immigration in the United States: A Time Series Approach." *Review of Black Political Economy* 36 (3): 151–60.

Stevens, L., and T. Bean. 2007. *Critical Literacy Context: Research and Practice in the K-12 Classroom*. Thousand Oaks, CA: Sage.

Stewart, E. 2007. "Individual and School Structural Effects on African American High School Students' Academic Achievement." *High School Journal* 91: 16–34.

Sullivan, A. L. 2010. "Preventing Disproportionality: A Framework for Culturally Responsive Assessment." *NASP Communiqué* 39 (3): 213–14.

Tatum, A. 2005. *Teaching Reading to African American Adolescent Males: Closing the Achievement Gap*. Portland, ME: Stenhouse.

Tatum, A. 2006. "Engaging African American Males in Reading." *Educational Leadership* 63 (5): 44–49.

Tatum, A. 2008a. "Overserved or Underserved? A Focus on Adolescents and Texts." *English Journal* 98: 82–85.

Tatum, A. 2008b. "Toward a More Anatomically Complete Model of Literacy Instruction: A Focus on African American Male Adolescents and Texts." *Harvard Educational Review* 78 (1): 155–80.

Tatum, A., and G. Muhammad. 2012. "African American Males and Literacy Development in Contexts That Are Characteristically Urban." *Urban Education* 47 (2): 434–63. https://doi.org/10.1177/0042085911429471.

Texas Education Agency. 2009. *Texas Assessment of Knowledge and Skills: Answer Key*. Austin, TX: self-published.

Topor, D. R., S. P. Keane, T. L. Shelton, and S. D. Calkins. 2010. "Parent Involvement and Student Academic Performance: A Multiple Mediational Analysis." *Journal of Prevention and Intervention in the Community* 38: 183–97.

Troyna, B. 1987. "A Conceptual Overview of Strategies to Combat Racial Inequality in Education." In *Racial Inequality in Education*, edited by B. Troyna, 213–20. London, England: Tavistock.

Turney, K., and G. Kao. 2009. "Barriers to School Involvement: Are Immigrant Parents Disadvantaged?" *Journal of Educational Research* 102: 257–71.

US Census Bureau. 2012. *The Black Population in the United States*. Washington, DC: self-published.

US Department of Education. 2012. *Teaching Children to Read*. Washington, DC: self-published.

Vasquez, V., S. Tate, and J. Harste. 2013. *Negotiating Critical Literacies with Teachers: Theoretical Foundations and Pedagogical Resources for Pre-Service and In-Service Contexts*. New York: Routledge.

Waters, S., D. Cross, and T. Shaw. 2010. "Does the Nature of Schools Matter? An Exploration of Selected School Ecology Factors on Adolescent Perceptions of School Connectedness." *British Journal of Educational Psychology* 80: 381–402. https://doi.org/10 .1348/000709909X484479.

Watson, A., M. Kehler, and W. Martino. 2010. "The Problem of Boys' Literacy Underachievement: Raising Some Questions." *Journal of Adolescent and Adult Literacy* 53: 356–61.

Whitaker, D., C. Graham, S. G. Severtson, C. D. Furr-Holden, and W. Latimer. 2012. "Neighborhood and Family Effects on Learning Motivation among Urban African American Middle School Youth." *Journal of Child and Family Studies* 21: 131–38. https://doi.org/10.1007/s10826-011-9456-1.

White, H. 2009. *Increasing the Achievement of African American Males.* Virginia Beach: Virginia Beach City Public Schools.

Wisconsin Department of Public Instruction. 2007. *Culturally Responsive Practices in Schools: The Checklist to Address Disproportionality.* Madison, WI: self-published.

Wood, D., B. Kurtz-Costes, and K. E. Copping. 2011. "Gender Differences in Motivational Pathways to College for Middle Class African American Youths." *Developmental Psychology* 47 (4): 961–67.

Wood, S., and R. Jocius. 2013. "Combating 'I hate this stupid book!': Black Males and Critical Literacy. *Reading Teacher* 66: 661–69. https://doi.org/10.1002/trtr.117.

Woodson, C. G. 1933. *The Miseducation of the Negro.* New York: Associated Publishers of the United States of America.

Wright, L. 2008. "Parental Involvement Strongly Impacts Student Achievement." Durham: University of New Hampshire.

Wu, F., and S. Qi. 2006. "Longitudinal Effects of Parenting on Children's Academic Achievement in African American Families." *Journal of Negro Education* 75: 415–29.

Appendix A

SCATTERPLOT OF ASSESSMENT AT
PRETEST AND POSTTEST TIME PERIODS

Scatterplot of Assessment at Pretest and Posttest Time Periods

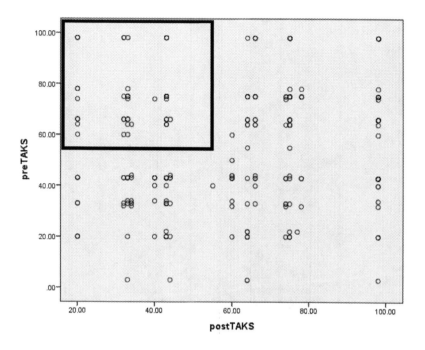

Appendix B

**CORRELATIONS BETWEEN THE PARENT
SURVEY AND READING SCORES**

Correlations between the Parent Survey and Reading Scores

Item Number on Survey	Pretest Full	Pretest Reduced	Posttest Full	Posttest Reduced
How often do you meet in person with teachers at your child's school?	-.03	-.02	.02	-.02
How involved have you been with a parent group(s) at your child's school?	-.02	.02	-.02	-.02
In the past year, how often have you discussed your child's school with other parents from the school?	-.02	-.02	.02	-.02
In the past year, how often have you helped out at your child's school?	.05	-.02	.02	-.02
How involved have you been in fundraising efforts at your child's school?	-.03	.00	.00	-.02
In the past year, how often have you visited your child's school?	.01	.04	.00	-.02
In the past year, how often have you communicated with the school about ways that you can help your child's learning at home?	-.03	-.03	.02	-.02
How often does your child struggle to get organized for school?	.00	.01	.01	-.02
How much effort does your child put into school related tasks?	-.02	.02	.01	-.02
When working on school activities at home, how easily is your child distracted?	-.04	-.03	.01	-.03
How regularly does your child read for fun?	-.04	.03	-.03	.01
How well does your child manage his or her emotions?	-.01	-.10	-.02	-.01
How often does your child give up on learning activities that he or she finds hard?	-.01	-.10	-.02	-.01
How motivated is your child to learn the topics covered in class?	-.04	-.05	.03	-.01
In general, how well does your child learn from feedback about his or her work?	-.03	-.00	.05	-.02
On average, how well does your child work independently on learning activities at home?	-.04	-.00	.06	-.01
What grade is your child in?	.01	.00	.03	.01

Appendix C

CORRELATIONS BETWEEN THE TEACHER CHECKLIST AND READING SCORES

Correlations between the Teacher Checklist and Reading Scores

Item Number on Checklist	Pretest		Posttest	
	Full	Reduced	Full	Reduced

Does the school culture support and celebrate diversity and view students of RCELD (racial, cultural, ethnic and linguistic diversity) as assets?

| | .20 | .09 | .13 | .16 |

Does the school have a positive behavioral support system for ALL students?

| | .02 | .10 | .13 | .16 |

Has the school principal established an attitude among staff that "all students are our students" as opposed to an attitude of "my students and your students"?

| | .03 | .12 | .14* | .19* |

Do teachers (e.g., general education, ESL, special education) work collaboratively to support all students?

| | .03 | .12 | .15* | .19* |

Are differentiated reading interventions (e.g., Title I, Read 180, Reading Recovery) available to students of RCELD?

| | .03 | .10 | .13 | .16* |

Has the school adopted a problem-solving approach that values assessment to drive instructional decisions?

| | .03 | .11 | .13 | .16 |

Do school teams receive sufficient administrative support when expressing concerns about meeting the needs of students of RCELD?

.00   .08   .13*   .13

Has the school established a multi-tiered model of intervention services?

-.00   .03   .07   .07

Do school teams actively consider other possible explanations (e.g., insufficient instruction, limited English proficiency, family risk factors) for the student of RCELD who has low achievement rather than automatically assuming a disability?

.03   .08   .11   .15

Does the Instructional Team actively consider whether absence or parent/family mobility of the student of RCELD negatively impacts continuity of general education classroom instruction?

.03   .10   .15*   .19

Has the Instructional Team made concerted efforts to reach out to parents/family members of students of RCELD by fostering collaboration, mutual trust, and respect?

.05   .07   .11   .13

Does the Instructional Team use peer supports in the classroom?

.03   .09   .11   .14

Does the Instructional Team incorporate culturally responsive materials and content in the curricula, and use culturally responsive teaching practices?

.03   .09   .03   .16*

Does the Instructional Team actively seek to identify the reason for a RCELD student's behavior, learning, or other difficulties?

.02   .09   .07   .12

Does the Instructional Team establish management practices by considering the impact of culture on school performance of a student of RCELD?

.06   .08   .10   .16*

Does the Instructional Team establish a classroom environment that accepts individual student differences and is positive, structured, and well managed?

.04   .09   .09   .16*

Does the Instructional Team set realistic, high expectations and standards for students of RCELD?

.02   .13   .11   .14

Are learning strategies explicitly taught to students of RCELD?

.05   .08   .04   .19*

Does the Instructional Team accommodate the needs of students of RCELD through differentiated instruction that reflects the interests and experiences of students of RCELD?

.02   .08   .12   .15

Printed in the United States
by Baker & Taylor Publisher Services